A Devotional

Out of the Quiet

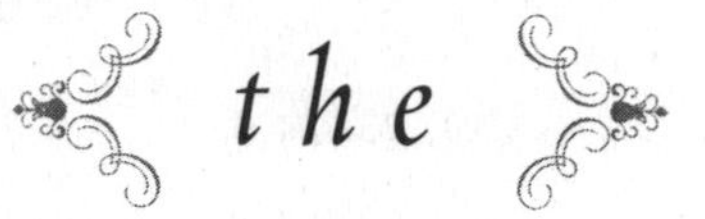

Responding to God's Whispered Invitations

Peter Wallace

NavPress®

Bringing Truth to Life

Our Guarantee to You

We believe so strongly in the message of our books that we are making this quality guarantee to you. If for any reason you are disappointed with the content of this book, return the title page to us with your name and address and we will refund to you the list price of the book. To help us serve you better, please briefly describe why you were disappointed. Mail your refund request to: NavPress, P.O. Box 35002, Colorado Springs, CO 80935.

The Navigators is an international Christian organization. Our mission is to reach, disciple, and equip people to know Christ and to make Him known through successive generations. We envision multitudes of diverse people in the United States and every other nation who have a passionate love for Christ, live a lifestyle of sharing Christ's love, and multiply spiritual laborers among those without Christ.

NavPress is the publishing ministry of The Navigators. NavPress publications help believers learn biblical truth and apply what they learn to their lives and ministries. Our mission is to stimulate spiritual formation among our readers.

ISBN 1-57683-596-0

Cover design by David Carlson Design
Cover image: Anthony Nagelman/Stone
Creative Team: Terry Behimer, Liz Heaney, Darla Hightower, Arvid Wallen, Pat Miller

Some of the anecdotal illustrations in this book are true to life and are included with the permission of the persons involved. In some cases the names have been changed. All other illustrations are composites of real situations, and any resemblance to people living or dead is coincidental.

Wallace, Peter M.
Out of the quiet : responding to God's whispered invitations / Peter Wallace.
p. cm.
Includes bibliographical references (p.) and index.
ISBN 1-57683-596-0
1. Christian life--Meditations. I. Title.
BV4501.3.W36 2004
242--dc22

2004002797

Printed in the United States of America

1 2 3 4 5 6 7 8 9 10 / 08 07 06 05 04

Contents

PART TWO

GOD INVITES YOU TO LIVE ABUNDANTLY

PART THREE

GOD INVITES YOU TO REACH OUT

Foreword

PETER WALLACE AND I share many things: the joy of being grandparents, a vocation to serve God through the national media, a fondness for *The Book of Common Prayer,* the oxymoronic estate of living in an urbanizing South, and a passionate enthusiasm for Eugene Peterson's *The Message*. It is this last one that tells the tale in these pages.

The Message is not so much a translation of the Bible—at least not in the customary sense of that word—as it is a para-translation. It is, in other words, a brilliant lifting up of the spirit and intent of our holy words out of the conventions and sometimes limiting contexts of their times into the becoming and appropriate conventions and idioms of our times. And so far as I know, no one has ever understood the nuances and pastoral uses of *The Message* as well as, much less better than, Peter Wallace.

In this volume of small pieces, Wallace has structured both a set and a system of devotions, using Peterson's para-translation as a vehicle and his own Christian experience as the way into consolation, obedience, worship, and wonder. Because of Wallace's efficient organization of these devotions into clear categories and sub-sets, any reader at any given moment can locate a Scripture and meditation that will inform and counsel the burdens, joys, or thoughts of that moment. Because of Wallace's acumen in selectively employing Peterson's work, every reader will be surprised into new understandings and appreciations of the foundations of the Christian life. And because of Wallace's quietness of voice, connecting the message and the unchanging truths of our faith to each other will be a delight to the heart of every reader.

And one last thing. Gentleness is not a virtue often touted in our times, but Peter Wallace is a gentle writer. Nothing is imposed here, nothing asserted in strident tones of insistence. Instead, all are welcome to sit a while and ponder. My suspicion is that that respite will make a difference in the life of most of those who do stop. But whatever the outcome, everyone who enters these pages will know himself or herself to have been engaged here; for Peter Wallace is a generous writer, as well as a gentle one.

Phyllis Tickle
The Farm in Lucy

Acknowledgments

THE AUTHOR WISHES TO thank the following for their extraordinary support:

Ramsay and Kathy Malcolm Hall
Harold and Kathryn McRae
Gray and Jean Temple
Gerry and CeCe Balboni
Larry and Pam Smith
Louis C. "Skip" Schueddig and the staff of the Episcopal Media Center
The trustees and staff of The Protestant Hour, Inc. / *Day 1*
All my good friends (you know who you are)
Aldred and Peggy Wallace, my parents
Edith Shock, my mother-in-law
My brothers and sister and their families
My son Matt, daughter Meredith, son-in-law Brandon, and grandson Tyler
And especially, my wife, Bonnie

These are the people who have . . .
provoked my thinking
encouraged my faith
accepted me
known me and still
love me.

Thanks also to:

Rebecca E. Price, my amazing agent and friend
Liz Heaney, my editor
Dan Rich and the staff of NavPress
Eugene Peterson, for his wonderful translation, *The Message*

What Is God Saying to You?

THE PROPHET ELIJAH WAS scared to death. His bold proclamations had landed him in deep trouble with the powers-that-be, and a furious Queen Jezebel had put a price on his head.

So Elijah ran for his life, all the way to the mountain of God, Mount Horeb, where he collapsed, exhausted, in a cave and slept.

Have you ever felt like that?

Worn out from the seemingly perpetual battle for survival in this world.

Aching for God's presence.

Frustrated that you have done so many of the right things with so little to show for it.

Yearning to hear God speak to you.

You may find, like Elijah, that sometimes God's message is right in front of you:

> Then the word of GOD came to him: "So Elijah, what are you doing here?"
>
> "I've been working my heart out for the GOD-of-the-Angel-Armies," said Elijah. "The people of Israel have abandoned your covenant, destroyed the places of worship, and murdered your prophets. I'm the only one left, and now they're trying to kill me."
>
> Then he was told, "Go, stand on the mountain at attention before GOD. GOD will pass by."

> A hurricane wind ripped through the mountains and shattered the rocks before GOD, but GOD wasn't to be found in the wind; after the wind an earthquake, but GOD wasn't in the earthquake; after the earthquake fire, but GOD wasn't in the fire; and after the fire a gentle and quiet whisper.
>
> When Elijah heard the quiet voice, he muffled his face with his great cloak, went to the mouth of the cave, and stood there. A quiet voice asked, "So Elijah, now tell me, what are you doing here?" (1 Kings 19:9-13)

My goal in these pages is to help you hear what God is saying, perhaps very quietly, to you today. I hope to help you train your spiritual ears to hear and respond to God's whispered invitations to experience life in all its fullness, as God generously beckons you to . . .

> come closer,
> live more abundantly, and
> reach out to others in God's name.

Throughout Scripture God expresses his desire to bring us closer into a divine embrace. I like how the Hadith Qudsi, the sayings of Prophet Muhammed, describes God's longing for us:

> If he draws near to Me a hand's span, I draw near to him an arm's length; if he draws near to Me an arm's length, I draw near to him a fathom's length. If he comes to me walking, I go to him running.[1]

God yearns for you. As we'll see in Scripture verse after verse, God beckons to you to *come closer*. God moves toward you at the smallest sign from you that you want more. God wants to experience a deeper, closer relationship with you through the Spirit who woos you.

Throughout Scripture God also invites you to *live abundantly*—to be as fulfilled and effective and blessed as possible in this life. When you discover who you really are as God's beloved creation, when you know how God's Spirit has gifted you, and when you embrace how God desires you to live, you will experience the abundant life God longs for you to live.

We'll also discover those invitations in Scripture in which God coaxes you to *reach out* to others. To serve someone in need, to speak an encouraging word, to share the blessing you have received with those around you.

As you embrace what God is saying to you out of the quiet, you'll no longer simply go through the motions or feel too tired to pray or read the Scripture or help someone in need. Instead, you'll grow increasingly hungry for more of God. Thirstier for a closer, more vibrant, more trusting, more empowered, and more fulfilling relationship with God.

It all starts with listening to what God is saying to you.

What Are You Saying to God?

This book will benefit you most if you are earnestly seeking the help it offers. That is, you have certain needs you want fulfilled—and you're asking God to fulfill them:

"God, I want to hear you speak to me."

Perhaps you are feeling frustrated because you can't hear God speaking personally to you, so you fail to achieve your spiritual potential. You live in a world whose distracting roar keeps you from hearing the "quiet whisper," so you feel a disconnect between God's Word and your everyday life in the real world.

Whether you're a seeker, taking initial steps in your pursuit of God, or a Christian who desires a fresh, true encounter with your Savior, this devotional book offers opportunities to hear what God is saying to you through invitations, admonitions, challenges, and commands from all of Scripture from Genesis to Revelation. Feel free to browse the contents page for a particular topic that speaks to you on any given day or focus on one reading a day. There is no right or wrong way to read this book. What's needed is a listening heart.

"God, I want to experience you more fully in my daily life."

The Bible is a big book full of stories and instructions for God's children to read, understand, and follow. It takes a lifetime to interact with it, apply it, and live it.

This book will help you focus on God's words to you day by day, so that you can accept the invitation to a deeper, richer relationship with God and with others.

In fact, the three sections—come closer, live abundantly, and reach out—follow the natural progression of our spiritual growth. It's a continuing cycle: getting closer to God's heart, discovering new ways to live fully and authentically in this world, and reaching out to others in service or support . . . and then starting all over again.

"God, I want a devotional resource that doesn't tell me what to believe, but introduces me to you and your Word and helps me work it all out myself."

You and I are on this journey together. We are continually trying to figure out our relationship with God and others. We are seeking to experience God more genuinely and then share that experience with each other.

So together, we'll interact with God's invitations, challenges, and admonitions to us from throughout Scripture. This is a devotional book, which means we won't be studying scholarly theories about Bible passages or debating fine points of theology. We won't be sidetracked by historical timelines or authorship controversies. Rather, we will take God's Word at face value and invite the Spirit to help us sense the grace, love, and power of God.

Are Your Ears Awake?

God wants to heal you. Fill you. Embrace you. Share with you. Encourage you. Challenge you. God wants you to live fully, joyfully, as a child of heaven and to live out that fullness by loving and serving others.

God wants all that for you, and more.

Experiencing it starts with a sensitive, listening heart, a willing spirit, an active mind. Jesus asks you,

> "Are your ears awake? Listen. Listen to the Wind Words,
> the Spirit blowing through the churches." (Revelation 2:29)

PETER WALLACE

Part One

God Invites You to

COME CLOSER

1

COME CLOSER

. . . AND TRUST GOD

> Know this well, then. Take it to heart right now: GOD is in Heaven above; GOD is on Earth below. He's the only God there is. (Deuteronomy 4:39)

YOU CAN STAKE YOUR life on this: The God you know, the God who knows you, is the One who lovingly rules the universe. This God beckons you to come closer.

You either trust this God or you trust nothing.

The substance of your faith rests on this.

So, when you are stewing in fear or stress or frustration about something going on in your life, or in the life of someone you love, ask yourself: Am I trusting God with this? Do I know well that there is a God in heaven and on earth who is in control, working in love and power and grace in the world?

When you study the newspaper headlines with trepidation and anxiety, concerned about the turmoil and hunger and hatred around the world, ask: Am I aware that God is the only God there is? Do I really trust this God? Am I willing to let this God use me to bring peace to my little corner of this world?

When you grieve over the serious illness or death of someone you love, examine your level of trust in God by asking: Do I believe in my heart of hearts that God is here with us? That we are with God forever? That God is doing what's good?

When you are pursuing behaviors or activities you know are not God's best for you—behaviors that are physically, emotionally, or spiritually unhealthy—ask: Am I acknowledging that God is present with me? Am I taking to heart the knowledge that I am God's beloved child?

Falsehood and doubt can threaten the vibrancy of your life with God and others. When you get down to it, how many people can you really, truly count on, no matter what? How many truths do you really know beyond all uncertainty?

Daily remind yourself of one truth, a truth on which you can stand, a truth you would do well to accept fully. No matter where you are in life or what you're dealing with, it can transform your experience:

"GOD is in Heaven above; GOD is on Earth below. He's the only God there is."

God, I believe in you. I trust you. I rest in you. At least I say I do. Help me to really mean it. To know it. To take it to heart. Amen. ■

2

COME CLOSER

. . . AND FACE THE ONE AND ONLY GOD

> "So turn to me and be helped—saved!—everyone, whoever and wherever you are. I am GOD, the only God there is, the one and only." (Isaiah 45:22)

IT DOESN'T MATTER WHO you are, where you are, or what your circumstances may be, God invites you, yearns for you, to turn and face "the one and only" God.

True fulfillment in life starts by coming closer to God, which requires surrendering, giving up your own direction, your own solutions. Coming close means taking your eyes off your own resources, your pet possessions, your well-constructed self-protective devices, and turning. Facing—looking right at—God.

This command—"turn to me"—is so simple, so clean. Yet we resist coming close to God, don't we? Our stubbornness keeps our neck aimed in the wrong direction, away from the God who yearns for us.

But what will happen if we turn and look to God?

We will be helped. Saved!

The word *saved* has, unfortunately, become a bit of a cliché in the Christian faith. The Hebrew root here, *yasha*, has some refreshing nuances. *Strong's Concordance* defines this word: "to be open, wide or free, that is, to be safe; causatively to free or succor . . .

defend, deliver . . . help, preserve, rescue, be safe, bring . . . salvation, . . . get victory."

Doesn't that describe what you yearn for? Isn't that what you desperately chase? Aren't you driving yourself to exhaustion with your craving for it?

God says:

"Look to me and be:

open,
wide,
free,
safe,
and victorious."

Only in God—the "only God there is"—can you experience this salvation; only in God can you find fulfillment for all time and beyond.

What is keeping you from turning, or turning again?

God, I turn to you. I run to you. I lean on you. I trust you and you alone for all the help and salvation I need. Amen. ■

3

COME CLOSER

. . . AND BECOME GOD'S FRIEND

> Become friends with God; he's already a friend with you. How? you say. In Christ. God put the wrong on him who never did anything wrong, so we could be put right with God.
> (2 Corinthians 5:20-21)

HOW DO YOU BECOME friends with God?

Think about the friends in your life. Recall how you met them. What were the circumstances? How did you feel when you met them? How did your friendship grow stronger: Did you immediately click or did it take some time?

So many friends come to my mind . . . some have come in and gone out of my life. Others have been part of my circle of support for many years. Still others I'm only just getting to know.

What are the common denominators that draw people together in friendship?

- An immediate acceptance of each other.
- A chemistry of mutual interests.
- A lively desire to get to know each other better.
- A yearning to do things together—fun or work or ministry or just life.
- A willingness to work through difficult times together.
- An eagerness to help each other out.

- An amazing weaving together of the hearts through open, honest communication with each other, often as a result of standing together through very difficult times.

Review this list carefully—it describes how God feels about you. Which of these characteristics describes your relationship with God? Which ones don't? What is keeping you from experiencing those qualities in your friendship with God?

The Bible is full of examples of people who became God's friends. Moses was called a friend of God, for "GOD spoke with Moses face-to-face, as neighbors speak to one another" (Exodus 33:11). About David God said, "He's a man whose heart beats to my heart, a man who will do what I tell him" (Acts 13:22). In 2 Corinthians 5:20-21, the apostle Paul declares that the Lord already considers himself your friend.

Does it seem a little trifling to think of your relationship with God as a friendship? After all, God is so much more—the Creator and Redeemer and Sustainer of the universe.

Yes, that's true—and God also wants you to come closer. God wants your friendship.

Like Moses and David, you can experience a deep friendship with God. Accept the invitation to experience the lifelong love, camaraderie, fulfillment, and purpose that come from being God's close friend.

God, thank you for the friends you have brought into my world, those who have enriched my life in the past and those who continue to do so now. Help me keep my primary relationship with you, my closest friend, growing and vibrant and mutually enjoyable. Help me to get to know you better so that my heart may beat as yours. Amen. ■

4

COME CLOSER

. . . AND WAIT FOR GOD

"Climb higher up the mountain and wait there for me; I'll give you tablets of stone, the teachings and commandments that I've written to instruct them." (Exodus 24:12)

ERNEST SHACKLETON UNDERSTOOD WHAT it means to "climb higher . . . and wait." He and his crew sailed for the South Pole in their ship, the *Endurance*, in August 1914. The crew of twenty-seven planned to make history as the first humans to cross Antarctica.

But the harsh realities of the Antarctic soon threatened not only the mission, but also their very lives. Early on, the *Endurance* became trapped in the ice, where it remained stuck for ten months—before the ice crushed the wooden vessel. The men lived on the ice floe for the next five months, and then left in lifeboats.

They made it to Elephant Island, but it was lifeless and deserted. Alone on the rocky, icy island, they were desperate for help. So Shackleton set out with five others in a lifeboat as a last-ditch attempt at survival. While the remaining crewmen waited, they hoped to make it to South Georgia Island, a base for whaling operations. It was eight hundred miles away.

Miraculously, they made it, but unfortunately they landed on the uninhabited side of the island.

There's a heart-stopping scene in a motion picture account of their adventures in which these crewmembers are forced to hike across the desolate island. Their supplies, food, and wits exhausted, they believe that if they can climb over a mountain standing between themselves and the whalers' supply outpost, they will be well on their way home. The climb is treacherous and challenging. Slowly they inch their way up the rough, icy, windswept mountain.

The summit looms into view—they are nearly there. But when they finally reach the top and look beyond, they see stretching into apparent infinity a range of similarly threatening mountains—twenty-six miles' worth of mountains—which have to be crossed if they are to survive.

They could easily have given up right then and died. But even though their hope was shattered, they kept on, tackling one mountain at a time, waiting, waiting to reach their goal.

When you have to wait, when things take longer or are more difficult or turn out differently than you expected, you can begin to doubt. You can stop trusting God.

Life is full of such times.

You spend difficult years in school pursuing your life dreams, only to find that the reality of the world affords little in the way of perfection when it comes to job or career.

You work hard at making your friendships, marriage, and family as positive and real as you can, and yet your struggles and conflicts only seem to deepen.

You plan and fret and work hard to make ends meet, and then a major unexpected expense blindsides you.

You study, pray, and sacrifice in an effort to grow closer to God, to build your faith and trust, and only feel a growing distance that seems impossible to breach.

During such times, "Climb higher . . . and wait."

When you accept the invitation to come closer and trust God during such times, your faith can become solid, unshakable, mature. You come to know God as the One who will meet you, who will climb with you, and wait with you, and ultimately give you all you need.

Shackleton and his five crewmembers eventually succeeded in their incredible trek. With the boats sent to rescue those left on Elephant Island, his entire crew—all twenty-seven of them—survived their two-year ordeal. They navigated those impossible odds and got through. They made it home.

When you trust God, even when you are waiting, you, too, can move forward through incredibly challenging times and find your way home.

God, when I have climbed through life expecting something glorious, the last thing I want to do is wait. Give me patience. Build my trust. For I know that the result will be something I will cherish for the rest of my life. And forever. Amen. ■

5

COME CLOSER

. . . AND PAY ATTENTION

> Attention, Israel! GOD, our God! GOD the one and only! Love GOD, your God, with your whole heart: love him with all that's in you, love him with all you've got! (Deuteronomy 6:4-5)

I USUALLY CONSIDER ACCOUNTS of people who hear God speaking directly to them as extremely suspect. But I vividly remember a time years ago when I heard God speak to me. It wasn't an audible voice, but I clearly "heard" the words spoken in love to my distressed mind.

At the time I was upset about the downward trend of a friendship. My best friend and I had spent lots of time together in church and at play—praying together, hiking together, eating lunch together, just being brothers together. But other relationships and responsibilities were claiming more and more of his time. I was clearly becoming too anxious and dependent, and he was reacting to my neediness, perhaps unconsciously, by putting even more distance between us. As a result, I wasn't much fun to be around, so he only avoided me more, which further fed my fear.

It was a frustrating cycle of pain, and it consumed far too much of my attention and energy.

One morning I cried out to God, begging for a change in my friend's attitude so we could go back to the way we were. After all, wasn't I a terrific person? Why didn't my friend appreciate me as he should?

That I could hear God in the midst of that is a miracle in itself. But the words came clearly into my mind, like clean, fresh rainfall on dry, burning sand: *Let go of the fear, and the love will remain.*

When I heard those words, I nearly jumped out of my easy chair with the recognition that God was speaking to me, reassuring me, instructing me, and giving me hope. If I could be bold enough to let go of my fear, I would discover that our love and friendship would remain—and grow into a healthier relationship.

As I trusted what I sensed God was saying to me, I could feel myself relax. My anxiety dissolved into peace.

Over time, I sensed a new balance with this friendship, and what's more, I began to let go of fear in my other relationships, even my marriage.

Ironically, my friend moved away a year or two later. I'm surprised to admit we only talk to one another on the phone maybe twice a year, with a few e-mails thrown in for good measure.

Even so, we both continue to sense the strong connection. On a recent business trip to a city near where his family now lives, we were able to get together and spend some time catching up, praying for each other, enjoying each other's company. Just like old times.

In the meantime, God has brought more love into my life through my family and new friends. So no matter how you look at it, the word I heard was true.

Maybe God is trying to tell you something in the midst of your fear or doubt or sadness. Listen. Pay attention to what God is saying to you. What you hear could change your life.

God, open my ears and my heart to the whisper of your Spirit. Help me to come closer to you by paying attention to the way you work in my life. Help me to love you with all I've got. Because you are the one and only. Amen. ■

6

COME CLOSER

. . . AND EXPERIENCE GOD'S LOVE

> "Pay attention, come close now,
> listen carefully to my life-giving, life-nourishing words.
> I'm making a lasting covenant commitment with you,
> the same that I made with David: sure, solid, enduring love." (Isaiah 55:3)

ON THE NIGHTS OUR grandson stays with us, I love watching my wife rock him to sleep, softly singing love songs to him. Tyler relaxes blissfully in Bonnie's arms, totally satisfied, surrendering to the rest he needs after an incredibly busy day of play.

That warm and wondrous image comes to mind when I read this verse about God singing a song of covenant love over us. In this music of the heavens, God pledges to love us with a faithful, committed, unyielding, everlasting love—a love even deeper than the love of a parent or grandparent.

Do you hear your Lord's love song? He wants you to. What he said to Isaiah and David he says to us. "Pay attention. Come close, and experience true renewal."

I witnessed the power of God's love song one Sunday morning in church. During our prayer time, the prayer leader always provides an opportunity for people in the congregation to speak out a word, phrase, or image that the Spirit brings to mind. It might be anything from "I see an image of a flowering tree" to "pain in the shoulder" to "a burning stick" or "a wheat field." If people sense that the word or image applies to them, they can consider it as an invitation from God to come forward for prayer with a prayer team of two or three members. Each prayer team invites the person to focus on God and receive whatever God would have for him or her—a word, some reassurance or direction, a sense of renewed strength.

One morning when I was serving on a prayer team, a woman who was clearly in emotional despair approached. I wondered if she could even focus her mind in prayer, she seemed so distracted and tense. She explained that one of the words someone had spoken out—something that probably meant nothing to the person who said it—had resonated within her spirit.

While we prayed for her, she stood there, a seeming wad of pain and fear. While the rest of the congregation took communion, the choir sang softly. They began to sing, "There is a balm in Gilead . . . to soothe the sin-sick soul." Immediately my prayer partner and I could sense the peace and presence of God infusing the woman, her muscles relaxing, her nerves untangling. Tears came to her eyes, a smile to her face, a glow to her countenance.

After a few moments of experiencing the loving, healing, reassuring presence of God, she blinked a few times, her face beaming. She said, "I am loved after all. I didn't even realize I needed that reassurance until God invited me to receive it." She hugged us and added, "That hymn they sang was my mother's favorite—she used to sing it to me all the time when I was a child." Smiling, she returned to her seat.

This woman paid attention to God's wooing to her and because she did, she heard the heavenly love song of grace and forgiveness.

When we hear God's love song, God lights a fire of renewal in our soul that cannot be extinguished by the wind, but only roars hotter, purer, with life and light and energy in that wind of the Spirit.

Its warmth spreads to everyone around us.
God's love gives life and nourishes the soul. Forever.
Can you hear it? Come close. Listen carefully.

God, I am heeding your invitation to come close, to listen carefully, to hear your loving, life-giving, spirit-renewing words. Help me experience your sure, solid, everlasting love. Amen. ■

7

COME CLOSER

. . . AND OBEY GOD ALONE

"No other gods, only me. No carved gods of any size, shape, or form of anything whatever, whether of things that fly or walk or swim. Don't bow down to them and don't serve them because *I* am GOD, your God, and I'm a most jealous God, punishing the children for any sins their parents pass on to them to the third, and yes, even to the fourth generation of those who hate me. But I'm unswervingly loyal to the thousands who love me and keep my commandments." (Exodus 20:3-6)

WHEN MOSES SHARED THE Ten Commandments, the Israelites were surrounded by a plethora of gods, usually based on some sort of animal form, typically cruel and bloodthirsty, terrorizing their deluded followers. Made by human hands, these gods were utterly powerless. Yet, the Israelites constantly went after them, looking for something better.

But whether the false god they worshiped was a fish or a bull or a bird or even some sort of demon, what could they have gained from it, other than some deluded sense of power or self-determination? How would they have benefited from serving a handmade knick-knack that held them in abject fear?

Why not instead pursue a relationship with the Creator God, the One who rules the universe? The One who expressed unyielding love and limitless care, who was committed to providing for every need, who promised an everlasting kingdom? The One who communicated with them, beckoning them to a full life? The One who would be "unswervingly loyal" to those who chose to love in return?

Which would you choose? Most of us would say the choice is obvious. Simple. Clear. No other gods for me, only God.

But then we turn our eyes away from that God we just committed to, and look at the job that could bring us fame.

Or the person we hope can meet our needs.

Or the financial opportunity that we think can take care of all our wants.

Or the reckless activity that promises to ease our pain.

Or the new car that we believe can make us feel more important, more accepted, more cool.

Or some other false, powerless, empty promise. Some other god.

God beckons to you: "No other gods, only me." How will you answer that invitation?

God, I hear your invitation to loyal commitment—to a relationship that matters. I want to obey. Make me mindful of the times I choose to worship things—empty, powerless, useless things—other than you. Amen. ■

1-28-07
Father God, help me to not place the desire for a different job ahead of you + me. I'm asking for your blessing on this job @ Prairie. I pray that it be your will + in your plan for me. I pray that it will be an opportunity to glorify you!

8

COME CLOSER

. . . AND REVERENCE GOD'S NAME

"No using the name of GOD, your God, in curses or silly banter; GOD won't put up with the irreverent use of his name." (Exodus 20:7)

I ALWAYS GET A slightly perverse kick out of watching other passengers when riding the MARTA subway train from the Atlanta airport back to my office. As people get on the train, one of the first things many of them do is pull out their cell phones and make a call. The train travels above ground for a few stops, and then plunges under downtown Atlanta for several more miles. And with the plunge into underground darkness, cell phones lose their signal, cutting off the conversations. I've heard many a passenger break this very commandment as a result.

A similar situation occurs when we flippantly use God's name: Our soul becomes disconnected from God.

Then, when we seriously call out to God, we feel a separation. The line is full of static or it's dead. The reality of God's presence is remote because we haven't been taking him seriously. God's name has become to us just another casual word, and so our relationship becomes just as casual and unimportant.

That's why God says, "Please don't. Instead, revere my name. Take it seriously. Don't cheapen it."

God expects our reverence, our sober acknowledgment of who he is. So make God's name mean something to you. Use it to worship, to adore, to praise, to sing, to pray, to share.

If you do, you'll keep your connection with God strong and alive.

God, I want to honor you as God of the universe, God of my life. Keep me sensitive and reverent. I want to keep the connection open and strong between us. I know you'll do your part; help me do mine. Amen. ■

9

COME CLOSER

. . . AND ENTER INTO GOD'S REST

"Observe the Sabbath day, to keep it holy. Work six days and do everything you need to do. But the seventh day is a Sabbath to GOD, your God. Don't do any work—not you, nor your son, nor your daughter, nor your servant, nor your maid, nor your animals, not even the foreign guest visiting in your town. For in six days GOD made Heaven, Earth, and sea, and everything in them; he rested on the seventh day. Therefore GOD blessed the Sabbath day; he set it apart as a holy day." (Exodus 20:8-11)

I GREW UP NEAR the end of the era of blue laws, which required the closing of virtually all commercial businesses on Sunday. My parents, good Methodists that they were, enforced their own blue laws. For instance, I knew that if I managed to avoid cutting the grass on Saturday, I wouldn't have to mow on Sunday.

Still, one of the most painful experiences of my youth came out of my folks' desire to observe the Sabbath. I was briefly infatuated with a cute blonde in our church youth group, and along with a few other teens I was hanging out with her one Sunday afternoon. A spontaneous group decision emerged to go catch a movie at the downtown theater. I stopped by my home on the way to get some money and permission, but was blindsided when my mom informed me I wasn't allowed to see a movie on a Sunday.

As my friends drove off without me, I was left fuming and embarrassed, my heart crushed by what I considered to be a ridiculous restriction. Now, of course, I can see better the wisdom behind the decision.

Over the years blue laws have pretty much disappeared from the books, and Sunday has become just another day in our week. Even personally it's harder than ever to obey God's command to set apart one day of the week for holy rest. The Sabbath has become just another weekend day to catch up with all the to-dos. Get some work done around the house. Run the errands that the busy workweek has prevented from getting done.

Without rest, our souls get exhausted.

Jesus made it clear: The Sabbath exists not for God's sake, but for our own. Your Lord beckons you to set aside a day each week to pray, to meditate, to *be*. God yearns for you to gather with brothers and sisters in worship and fellowship, in learning and contemplation. God desires that you spend some time with yourself, your family, and your Lord.

The Sabbath provides an opportunity for rest and renewal, an invitation to communion and contemplation. Our observance of the Sabbath allows God to heal and strengthen souls made weary by six days of life in this world.

Are you getting the rest you need? Take some time today to reflect on how you can set aside a day each week for rest and renewal—and then do it.

God, help me obey your call for a day set aside to focus on you, by myself and with my fellow believers. Give me the wisdom to prioritize and reorganize my activities so I can live in obedience. Thank you for the refreshing renewal you promise as a result. Amen. ■

10

COME CLOSER

. . . AND HONOR YOUR PARENTS

"Honor your father and mother so that you'll live a long time in the land that GOD, your God, is giving you." (Exodus 20:12)

THIS COMMANDMENT COMES WITH a promise: When we value our parents and their love and care for us, when we esteem them and revere them as a God-given source of wisdom and provision, then our life will be rich and full.

Of course, not all parents follow God's calling to raise their children in life-giving ways. You may have strongly negative feelings about your parents because they abused you emotionally or even physically. Even so, your parents gave you life, and you can honor them by praying for them, by doing your best to understand them, and by forgiving them.

Regardless of the parents we had, most of us have rebelled against them to some degree as a way of separating ourselves and becoming more autonomous. I'm no different, though my rebellion was relatively tame.

Still, in recent years, I have come to appreciate my folks' views and beliefs once again, thanks in part to the gift of hindsight. I can see that their occasional disapproval of some of my early decisions in life arose out of their concern that I become my own person, to be sure, but also happy, balanced, fulfilled, and secure.

My parents are now in their autumn years, and I seek to honor them by regularly e-mailing or calling them, listening to them, telling them I love them, and visiting them when I can. How I wish I could do that more often! I find I have never appreciated or loved them more than I do now.

Now that I'm the father of grown children, I understand my folks' parental concern for me, particularly in my young adult years. It's one thing to be concerned about the safety of young children. But when they are older, their choices potentially have much more serious consequences—even of life and death.

It's not always easy, but as a parent I try not only to provide my children with clear, godly direction for living, but to honor their freedom and encourage their individual growth and fulfillment. When I do, they much more readily give me honor in return.

Which makes life more worth living for all of us in the land God has given us.

God, give me wisdom and understanding to enable me to honor my parents in positive, appropriate ways. Above all, help me to honor you, my heavenly Father, the source of all wisdom and goodness and love. Amen. ■

11

COME CLOSER

. . . AND OBEY GOD IN YOUR RELATIONSHIPS

"No murder.
No adultery.
No stealing."
(Exodus 20:13-15)

WHEN IT COMES TO murder, adultery, and stealing, God's Word is simple, clear, and direct: No.

Libraries upon libraries of books could be written recounting the painful, devastating human history that has resulted from willfully breaking these commands—or ignoring them or casually slipping away from them.

Some read these words and nod smugly, thinking, *I've never killed anybody or broken my marriage vows. And that time I stole a pack of gum from the grocery store? Every kid does that! That didn't mean anything.*

Others have suffered the consequences of breaking these laws. They have discovered firsthand that these are important values upon which civilization rests.

But Jesus says we're all guilty. In the Sermon on the Mount (see Matthew 5) he contended that even *thinking* about murdering someone, or lusting in your heart over another, or considering what it would be like to have something that's not yours, is just as serious a breach of God's will as the actual act itself.

Jesus wasn't trying to load us up with feelings of powerlessness over our own lusts, but to force us to look to him for help, for relief, for true power. While these commandments point to our absolute inability to obey them by ourselves, they also point to the complete provision God has given us through Christ to satisfy them. So they're not restrictions so much as revelations of true freedom, safety, and security.

They speak an invitation: Come closer. Let God forgive and cleanse you for your past failures. Receive the power to live a healthy, positive, obedient life. Experience within these protective boundaries the true fulfillment and shameless freedom and security that only God can give.

God, help me to hear your "no" in a positive light. Help me to see it as an invitation to come closer to your way. Help me to lean on Christ and his righteousness, to call on the Spirit's power, to stay safe and secure within the boundaries of your love. Amen. ■

12

COME CLOSER

. . . AND SPEAK ONLY THE TRUTH

"No lies about your neighbor." (Exodus 20:16)

UNFOUNDED GOSSIP HURTS. Some years ago when he was still single, I often had lunch with a close friend. We hadn't seen each other for a while because he'd been out of town, so we'd arranged to meet at a pizza place not far from where he worked at a large high-tech manufacturing facility.

My friend had taught me that brothers are allowed to hug one another, which was a wonderful revelation for me. Early in our friendship, I stuck my hand out for him to shake after seeing him at church—a normal farewell. He looked at my hand, then said with a smile, "We hug."

So, typically, we did hug each other whenever we met. But my friend often hesitated hugging me whenever we met in a public place outside of church. Still, on that particular day we hadn't seen each other in a while, so we had our arms around each other's shoulders as we walked toward the restaurant. We laughed our way into the restaurant and enjoyed our lunch together. Afterward we hopped into our cars and headed back to our separate jobs.

The next day in a phone conversation he announced, "No more hugging in public."

"How come?" I asked, more than a bit perplexed.

"Well, there were some people from my office at the pizza place who saw us hugging in the parking lot. The word has spread around here like wildfire that I'm gay!"

As a single man in his thirties, my friend was particularly sensitive to this false assertion. So that ended that. But why did it even matter? I suppose when he got married a year or so later the rumors died down, but who knows.

God says don't spread lies or even rumors about your neighbor. Don't start them; don't spread them. Not just about your literal neighbor, that word can refer to any close associate, including brother or sister, companion, friend, or spouse.

Underneath the surface layer of this commandment, we find an underlying truth. God invites us to a life of transparency and honesty, to relationships built on trust, justice, and charity.

What does that look like?

It means not avoiding confrontation, not holding back, but telling the truth carefully, honestly, with a view to building up rather than tearing down.

It means not stifling your own difficulties, fears, doubts, or negative feelings, but being honest about them and dealing with them positively, on your own or with appropriate help.

It means seeking out others whose words or actions may have hurt you—not to pay them back, but to discuss the matter with the goal of reconciliation.

It means living without worrying about whether others will accept you or whether you'll be considered successful or good. It means just being yourself as God created you.

God invites you to come closer by building a heart of obedience. God calls to you: Live the truth. Be the truth.

God, keep me honest. Transparent. Trustworthy. Truthful.
Help me to build up my neighbor, not tear him or her down.
In the power of your Spirit. Amen. ■

13

. . . AND OBEY GOD IN YOUR HEART

"No lusting after your neighbor's house—or wife or servant or maid or ox or donkey. Don't set your heart on anything that is your neighbor's." (Exodus 20:17)

I HAD TROUBLE WITH this commandment when I was a kid. But that was really Phil's fault.

Phil lived four houses down from me. All the other homes on our avenue were stately dark brick, two stories with large porches. My house was a Methodist parsonage, but you wouldn't notice much difference between it and all the other homes along the avenue, except for Phil's house. His home stuck out like a beautifully manicured thumb: a modern brick ranch with huge windows and a cool semicircular driveway.

Phil had his own huge bedroom; I had to share mine with one of my brothers. His home had all the most modern amenities, even an automatic dishwasher. He had a color TV before just about anyone else did. But that was nothing. Inside the home, in a contemporary, white-graveled courtyard, a beautiful bronze fountain shot both water and flame into the air in an amazing elemental dance.

You can imagine how that impressed my eight-year-old self.

Phil was a year older than I. I don't remember playing much with him by myself; usually Phil was just part of the neighborhood gang, which included my two best friends both named David.

How many games of touch football, baseball, and every form of tag known to humanity did we play in Phil's wide-open yard? How many evenings did we spend chasing lightning bugs in his big corner lot? How many lazy afternoons did we spend at his house, checking out his latest comic books or playing with his amazing new toys?

Sometimes we'd go camping on wooded property owned by Phil's father. We'd go to sleep around a dying campfire in worn-out Boy Scout sleeping bags (except for Phil; his was brand new).

At age sixteen, when he got his driver's license, Phil's parents gave him a brand-new Jeep. The rest of us had to borrow our parents' definitely uncool old Chryslers and Chevrolets to get around, and even that was a rare privilege.

Oh, how I hated Phil. How I lusted after his possessions. He had everything a boy could ever want or need, and then some. If you had looked in heaven's post office, my mug would have been plastered on the Wanted poster for breaking the Tenth Commandment time and again, because of Phil.

I lost track of Phil in college, but years later I learned the shocking rest of the story from a family member. Phil had had three failed marriages and early on had become an alcoholic, which caused his liver to shut down when he was only forty-three. Phil was my first peer to die.

His tragic story reminds us that possessions don't make us happy. They don't soothe the ache in our souls. In fact, sometimes the things we think will bring us satisfaction are the very things that will keep us from it.

No matter who you are, no matter what you have, remember this: God has provided, and will provide, everything you need to be content and fulfilled. You are complete in God. You don't need to lust after what someone else has, because if you don't have it, God must know you don't need it.

Can you trust that? Can you trust God?

Shift your eyes from your neighbors to your God. And keep them there.

God, my life is complete in you. You are the provider of all that I need. Help me to come closer to you, to keep my eyes on you, trusting your provision. In this world, that can be a tall order. But you're an all-powerful God. Amen. ■

14

. . . AND HEAR GOD'S CALL

> After all these things, this word of GOD came to Abram in a vision: "Don't be afraid, Abram. I'm your shield. Your reward will be grand!" (Genesis 15:1)

SOMETIMES EVEN WHEN WE are doing what we were created to do, the pressures and responsibilities of life can wear us down, empty us of hopeful energy, and fill us with the fear that it's only going to get worse.

Just ask Abram. That's apparently how he felt. God's gentle, encouraging words to him in this verse reveal that Abram must have had some doubts or fears about what still lay ahead "after all these things."

What "things"? Flip back a few chapters for the answer.

- God calls Abram to abandon the status quo—life in Ur—and launch out into the unknown at the word of a God few people really knew much about. (Genesis 12:1)
- God gives this aging man the seemingly impossible task of founding a nation. (Genesis 12:2-3)
- Abram and Lot, Abram's somewhat selfish nephew, deal with a lot of unsavory characters already living in this land that had supposedly been given to him. (Genesis 12:4—13:18)

- Abram gathers a band of three hundred and eighteen men and rescues his nephew from a consortium of warring kings. (Genesis 14)

Abram survived all this and more in order to answer God's call on his life, but despite clear evidence that he was doing what God wanted him to do, he still felt some negative emotions about what was ahead.

He had been a wealthy, successful, yet simple man when God called him to step out and do something astonishingly dramatic with the promise of a magnificent nation and eternal glory. He's in between what he left and what God has promised, and in the midst of the apparent chaos, God reassures Abram with the words of the opening verse.

Can you relate with how Abram felt? Are you doing what God has called you to do? Stepping out boldly, trustingly, into God's life purpose for you, yet unsure of what the future holds? If so, God's inviting words to Abram are also God's words for you:

"Don't be afraid. I'm your shield. Your reward will be grand!"

Or are you ensconced comfortably in Ur? Is God calling you to do something that you are afraid to do or go somewhere that you are resistant to go? God is also saying to you:

"Don't be afraid. I'm your shield. Your reward will be grand!"

God, it's clear that the vast responsibility and the unexpected incidents in his life would have overwhelmed Abram if he didn't trust you with his whole heart. I admire the results of his obedience. And I yearn for that same level of faith. Help me sense your calling, your presence, your power, so that I can step out without fear knowing you are my shield. Amen. ■

15

COME CLOSER

. . . AND ENCOUNTER GOD'S HOLINESS

> God said, "Don't come any closer. Remove your sandals from your feet. You're standing on holy ground." (Exodus 3:5)

SEVERAL YEARS AGO A couple of brothers in the faith and I were walking up a hilly, wooded path to a rock outcropping, an expanse of gray granite that topped a hill bordering Camp Mikell, a church camp in northeast Georgia. We'd been participating in a men's weekend retreat that had just wrapped up. But on this Sunday afternoon as the participants left to return to the bustle of the city, my friends and I wanted to pause and simply be in God's presence for a little while longer before hitting the road.

So we walked up the path and sat on the sun-warmed granite to gaze at the lush green valley below and around us. It was sunny, though enormous puffy clouds occasionally dimmed the solar blaze. A faint breeze embraced us. To the right we could see the large wooden cross witnessing to the valley from another hilltop within the campgrounds. Ahead of us, we could catch glimpses of the nearby llama farm and hear the animals' unique bleats.

Other than those bleats, the soothing swish of tree leaves dancing in the breeze, and the occasional birdsongs, all was quiet.

This is a holy place, I thought. *God is real. God is here, almost tangibly present. And God's presence makes this place special and hallowed.* I felt so close to God's holy presence that I took off my hiking boots. My friends sensed my purpose and did the same. Then we stretched out on the warm rock face and in conversational prayer talked with God about each other and our loved ones.

Have you ever had a similar experience? Have you ever had a strong sense of God's holy presence—even in a place you never expected it?

Moses had been minding his own business as a shepherd when God beckoned to him to come closer, through the astonishing sight of a scrub bush that flamed with fire without being consumed.

God's fiery presence made earth and rock pure and holy and glorious. God's perfect reality redeemed the creation. But Moses had been wandering among the dust and dirt of idolatrous humanity, and he had to remove his soiled sandals so that God could deal directly with his heart. Cleansing it. Filling it. Releasing it from pain and fear and uncertainty to find its destiny in the will of God.

Mighty things can happen when you encounter the holy presence of God. During a private retreat a few years later, I returned to that same rocky outcropping at Camp Mikell and again removed my hiking boots. During my time alone, God's holiness broke through to shatter my spiritual complacency and soften my heart, allowing the Spirit to work. I didn't know what the future held for me, but I did know I was ready for God to lead me into it.

Once again, that mountainside had become holy ground for me, and perhaps I caught a fleeting sense of what Moses himself had felt on his holy ground.

Where is your holy ground? It's wherever you sense God's presence—a presence that spurs you to radical obedience. It might be a rocky hillside or a peaceful valley. Or perhaps where you are right now is your holy place because you sense God is there with you as a burning bush or a gentle breeze or a tender touch.

Remove your shoes and worship. Listen to God's Spirit wooing you. Mighty things can happen through you as a result of this supernatural encounter with holiness.

God, I sense you with me now. Your Spirit burns within my heart. You call me into your holy presence to come as close as I possibly can. I worship you. I kneel before you. I trust you. Amen. ■

16

. . . AND TALK TO GOD

"This is your Father you are dealing with, and he knows better than you what you need. With a God like this loving you, you can pray very simply. Like this:

'Our Father in heaven,
Reveal who you are.
Set the world right;
Do what's best—
as above, so below.
Keep us alive with three square meals.
Keep us forgiven with you and forgiving others.
Keep us safe from ourselves and the Devil.
You're in charge!
You can do anything you want!
You're ablaze in beauty!
Yes. Yes. Yes.'" (Matthew 6:8-13)

JESUS INVITES US TO pray like he did. Simply. Knowing that God our Father knows us better than we know ourselves, and he knows exactly what's best for us in every area of our life—and the life of all of creation.

So why do we complicate the matter? Why do we attend seminars and read weighty tomes on prayer? Not that those things will hurt us or hinder our ability to pray. But sometimes we feel the need to figure it all out before we even try.

Other times we simply don't feel like praying. We can't seem to put two prayerful words together in any way that makes sense.

What does God say to us during such times?

Many years ago following particularly rough times with my career, church, friends, family, and even God, it was difficult for me to draw close to God. Prayer seemed impossible. I could hardly read the Bible. Such activities seemed meaningless and empty.

How could I pray to a God who had allowed such chaos into my life?

Slowly, tentatively, after long weeks passed, I began to be able to talk to God about how I was feeling and about what was happening. My words were simple, direct, honest.

Now I look back on that time as essential in my own spiritual growth. By persisting in coming close to God through prayer, even when I didn't feel like it, I invited the Spirit to strip me of the faulty assumptions I had based my faith on. As a result, I could begin to build a relationship with God that was honest and true and admit that I will never have everything all figured out. And that is okay—it's no reason to draw apart from God.

If I had not gone through this tough time, I would probably still be living more of a shallow, false, superficial religion. I wouldn't have grown to where I am today—with such a long, long way still to go, yet with an experience of God as real as my relationship with my wife or my grandson.

Do you *feel* like praying today? Do you *feel* like coming close to God?

No matter how far away you may feel from God, you can draw close with a simple prayer, knowing that you are praying to a God who knows you completely and still loves you totally.

A God who hears you and knows what's best for you, now and in the long run.

Who yearns deeply for your company in open, honest, loving conversation.

Who can't wait to answer your prayers and work in abounding ways in your life.

Yes. Yes. Yes.

God, thank you that you know me thoroughly and accept me completely. Thank you for the privilege of prayer. I want to spend time with you now, talking things over, acknowledging your presence and provision. Amen. ■

17

. . . AND BE RENEWED

"Hey there! All who are thirsty,
come to the water!
Are you penniless?
Come anyway — buy and eat!
Come, buy your drinks, buy wine and milk.
Buy without money — everything's free!" (Isaiah 55:1)

DO YOU TAKE WATER for granted? After all, you have bottled water in your refrigerator, a water fountain at work, even kitchen tap water. At the slightest twinge of thirst, it's not difficult to satisfy the craving.

When was the last time you were really thirsty? On a hot summer day hiking in the woods with a canteen near empty? On a beach sizzling under the sun, too relaxed to be bothered to grab a chilly, sweaty can of soda? Working outside in biting, dry air, shoveling a thick blanket of snow? After eating a big Easter ham dinner, parched by the salty meat? But even in those times it probably didn't require much effort to slake your thirst.

Can you remember a time you were dying for a sip of water? Do you know what it means to thirst? Really?

While you ponder that question, ask yourself about your spiritual thirst. Are you thirsty for God? Does your dry, dusty spirit yearn for refreshment from God's hand, a fountain of living water bubbling within your soul?

That thirst may be much deeper than your physical thirst has ever been.

Sometimes we get so involved in our activities that we don't even realize how thirsty we are. Once when my wife, Bonnie, and I were keeping our grandson before he was two, he'd gone for a walk with Grandma, played outside, and then cavorted on our deck for a while, entertaining us with his nonstop, inquisitive, full-force investigations of every plant, leaf, and twig on the deck.

After a while Bonnie offered him a juice cup—and he grabbed it and drank heartily nonstop for several minutes. If he had been aware of his mighty thirst, he was unable to ask for what he needed, but he gladly took it when offered.

Spiritually, we often do something similar. We become so involved in the minutia of daily living that we don't realize how parched our soul really is—until the Spirit grabs hold of us in some surprising way and offers the cleansing, cooling, renewing draft of the holy water of God's presence. Nothing refreshes more.

Hear God's clear, cool invitation to you: "Come. Come to the water. Come, if you are thirsty, to the flowing, bubbling, effervescent fountain of eternal life."

Renewal flows from God alone. If you are thirsty, even the least bit, for spiritual reality, God invites you, welcomes you, yearns for you to come to the waters. To stop, in the midst of your busy day, and consciously drink in God's presence.

And that's just the start. When you come into God's presence through prayer and meditation, wine and milk will flow freely: the wine of the Spirit, the milk of God's mother-like love.

Best of all, God's spiritual refreshment costs nothing. It is up to you to come, receive, and be filled to overflowing with the invigorating nourishment only God can give you.

"Come," God invites. "Come thirsty and drink deeply."

God, I yearn for your renewing drafts of the water of life. Thank you for the invitation to come to you for your free gift of eternal life. Let me drink deeply. Amen. ■

18

COME CLOSER

. . . AND BE SPIRITUALLY NOURISHED

"Why do you spend your money on junk food,
your hard-earned cash on cotton candy?
Listen to me, listen well: Eat only the best,
fill yourself with only the finest." (Isaiah 55:2)

HAVE YOU EVER ATTENDED a really fancy banquet? I don't mean the rubber-chicken-serving community or church function. I mean a banquet with tables groaning under the weight of mouth-watering delicacies. Fine crystal and expensive china and exquisite silverware. Crisply attired servers attending to your every need as though they could read your mind. Beautiful music performed by a skilled chamber orchestra providing the perfect ambience for stimulating conversation.

Frankly, such experiences have been very rare in my life—although one sumptuous banquet I attended as a young newspaperman fresh out of college certainly qualifies. It was held at the extravagantly luxurious Greenbrier resort in West Virginia and attracted a wide range of business and political luminaries from across the state. But I was so overwhelmed by all the silverware, plates, and stemware surrounding my plate, that I ended up accidentally eating the wrong salad! I was certainly enjoying that fresh, tasty salad—until I realized with horror my egregious *faux pas*.

But such earthly banquets—extravagant though they may be—

fade into insignificance when we consider what God has prepared for you and me. God has set before us every good thing we could possibly imagine, and far more, and patiently waits to serve it to us. If only we would come.

But we may not even be aware of the feast prepared in our honor, awaiting our enjoyment. We're busy working, doing, moving about, laboring for a crust of hard bread or airy cotton candy.

We pass up even the most basic spiritual nourishment for junk food, and instead fill our craving with something false and empty and futile. Something that looks like it should taste good and fill our bellies with satisfaction, but it never can.

Maybe it's success in the business world. Money to buy all sorts of designer goods and valuable stuff. Status in a world of people always trying to outdo each other. Relationships that should soothe old pain and make hearts beat full forever, but oddly never quite do, so we try another type of junk food.

"Listen to me, listen well!" God cries to us, holding out an alternative. It is wholesome. Delightful. Rich. Fulfilling. It is the best: The spiritual feast made available to you in Jesus Christ is an endless and powerful and filling and pure and utterly satisfying banquet. We only need to come to the table.

Will you come?

God, in my relentless search for fulfillment, help me to come to you instead of to the things that never satisfy. Help me to realize that the banquet you've invited me to holds all the satisfaction, all the fulfillment, that I could ever hope to receive. Amen. ■

19

COME CLOSER

. . . AND FIND WHAT'S TRUE

GOD's Message to the family of Israel:
"Seek me and live.
Don't fool around at those shrines of Bethel,
Don't waste time taking trips to Gilgal,
and don't bother going down to Beer-sheba.
Gilgal is here today and gone tomorrow
and Bethel is all show, no substance." (Amos 5:4-6)

TIME AFTER TIME, GOD graciously, inexhaustibly, extended to Israel an invitation of mercy: "Seek me and live." Come home. Return to me and be welcomed. Forsake the false and find the true. Turn from death and experience true, fulfilling, everlasting life.

Yet, time after time, Israel spurned God's gracious wooing. They felt they knew how to live their lives more meaningfully, more successfully than their Creator did. So they wasted their time fooling around with meaningless, powerless idols. Ideas and approaches to life that were "all show, no substance." Empty and ultimately fruitless.

God wanted them—and wants you—to "seek me and live," because only God's presence can truly fulfill you.

What does seeking God look like?

The Hebrew root behind the word *seek* has the sense of diligence, of habit. It means to frequent a place. To walk around in it. Be in it. Search carefully in it.

So, you seek when you dwell in God's presence and make yourself at home in God's ways.

You seek by keeping God foremost in your thoughts, in your decision-making process, in your relationships with others, and as you fulfill your calling.

You seek by searching for ways to serve as a channel of God's love and care to those in need around you.

God-seeking takes courage. It requires taking responsibility. It means paying attention.

But seeking God is the best way to experience a life of true meaning, fulfillment, purpose, and joy.

God, give me the courage and intentionality I need to truly seek you, to keep seeking you, to stop looking for fulfillment in empty places. Thank you for continually wooing me to come into your presence. Amen. ■

20

COME CLOSER

. . . And Trust God Amidst Change

> Put into practice what you learned from me, what you heard and saw and realized. Do that, and God, who makes everything work together, will work you into his most excellent harmonies. (Philippians 4:9)

OVER THE YEARS MY son Matt and I enjoyed going camping several times, usually in a state park. One summer a few years ago when Matt was about to leave for college, we decided it would be good to get one more camping trip in before he left our family nest. Besides, we hadn't camped for a couple of years.

This time Matt didn't want to camp at one of those "wimpy" state parks with water faucets and restrooms and flat, prepared surfaces to pitch a tent on. He wanted a more primitive site. I thought of a favorite site in north Georgia where he and I had camped years before. It was a gorgeous wooded area just off the Richard Russell Scenic Highway.

As I recalled, you had to really know where you were going in order to find it because the forest service road wasn't marked. But once you found your way there, you'd have your choice of three or four nice campsites along the roaring creek. A nearby meadow offered a great vantage point to gaze at the stars at night. Across the creek and down a ways was the switchback trail that led to the spectacular Duke's Creek Falls.

So that's where we headed. We drove up around noon that Saturday and, armed with Internet maps, found the location again with no problem.

But things had changed.

The Duke's Creek area was apparently now part of the Raven Cliffs Wilderness Area and Smithgall Woods. The spot where we had camped a few years earlier was in the process of being changed, upgraded, with a new gravel parking lot, improved roads, and—I could hardly believe it!—restroom facilities.

Not only that, it had a new name. A fresh forest service sign—still partially covered with plastic because it wasn't officially ready yet—announced the site as the Raven Cliffs Trailhead.

I couldn't get my bearings. It was clearly the same place I remembered, but it looked and felt so different. Construction junk was piled everywhere. It was messy and confusing. I didn't like the changes.

But we pitched our tent on a large campsite right beside the rushing Duke's Creek. Only one other couple had chosen to camp in the area, and they were a good distance away from us. Nobody else showed up, probably because we had torrential thunderstorms that weekend. Matt and I enjoyed ourselves in spite of the rain.

Isn't that just like life? No matter how much we want things to remain the same, they change. We experience changes in our job, relationships, and circumstances. Inevitably change causes us to lose our bearings and feel uncomfortable.

But if we live determined to come ever closer to God, then we can be assured that, ultimately, the change will be for the better. The process may be confusing and messy and even painful. It can make us pine for the old ways of life and question God's good sense.

But, *"God, who makes everything work together, will work you into his most excellent harmonies."*

Someday we will look back at all the earth-shattering changes we have experienced and realize what happened to us and through us as a result of them, and we will see that it was good.

That's why I have a feeling that one day I'll head back to my favorite campsite by Duke's Creek and be able to enjoy the beauty of creation there—as well as the new restroom facilities.

God, thank you for the promise of obedient faith. I yearn to be part of your "most excellent harmonies," everything working together—even the drastic, confusing changes in life—for your glory. Amen. ■

21

COME CLOSER

. . . AND REKINDLE YOUR FIRST LOVE

"Do you have any idea how far you've fallen? A Lucifer fall! Turn back! Recover your dear early love. No time to waste, for I'm well on my way to removing your light from the golden circle." (Revelation 2:5)

IF JESUS WERE TO speak to me, I hope he would say positive, encouraging things: tell me what a great job I'm doing; acknowledge all the hard work I've put in on his behalf.

He said such things to the church at Ephesus. He told the apostle to send a letter to the church and to tell them: "I see what you've done, your hard, hard work, your refusal to quit. I know you can't stomach evil, that you weed out apostolic pretenders. I know your persistence, your courage in my cause, that you never wear out" (verses 2-3).

Clearly the believers at Ephesus were working together. They stood firmly for Christ, especially against those who promoted false and untrustworthy teachings. Unfortunately for the church at Ephesus, Jesus has a "but" for them: "But you walked away from your first love—why? What's going on with you, anyway?"

Ouch.

Yes, they may have been doing all the right things, but apparently they were doing them for the wrong reasons, in the wrong power. They'd walked away from their first love. They may have been doctrinally pure and argued well the fine points of the truth. But they weren't acting out of the regenerative love of Christ, the love that had wooed them into the fold in the first place.

Their goal had become to prove themselves right, to overcome views they considered wrong and harmful. They had lost sight of the main reason Jesus had come: to invite people into loving relationship with God, to bid them to love God with heart and soul and strength and mind, and their neighbors—all of them—as themselves.

I don't know about you, but Jesus' words make me uncomfortable. Like the Ephesians, I can point to all the right things I'm doing, but many times I do them out of self-promoting, self-protecting, self-righteous motivations. At times I too have fallen away from my first love.

Have you?

If so, these verses are a wake-up call to turn around and come closer to God once again. To reclaim that love that filled you to overflowing when you first met Jesus.

Is Jesus saying those words to you today?

If so, listen.

Reconsider your motives.

And recover your dear early love for him.

Jesus, it's so easy to get caught up in the responsibilities of being a Christian, and start fulfilling them in the wrong spirit, in my own power and wisdom. When I have gone too far in the wrong direction, please remind me to turn back and come closer once again. Thank you for beckoning me back to the early love you and I shared and for encouraging me to live out of that love in the present . . . and always. Amen. ■

22

COME CLOSER

. . . AND EXPERIENCE REST

> "Are you tired? Worn out? Burned out on religion? Come to me. Get away with me and you'll recover your life. I'll show you how to take a real rest. Walk with me and work with me—watch how I do it. Learn the unforced rhythms of grace. I won't lay anything heavy or ill-fitting on you. Keep company with me and you'll learn to live freely and lightly."
> (Matthew 11:28-30)

THESE ARE SOME OF the most beautiful words of invitation I have ever read. How I want to come closer and relax in Jesus' presence. How thirsty I am for his company, to be alone with him.

I haven't always felt this way. Going somewhere by myself just didn't seem to fit my personality. I love my wife, enjoy being with her and going places with her. I enjoy the company of good friends and family. How could I go somewhere by myself? Would I drive myself crazy? Would I be bored to tears, unable to do anything constructive, incapable of opening up to God?

Five years ago, during Lent, I decided to find out. I wanted to meet with God to get a fresh sense of direction for my life. So I arranged to stay in a cabin next to a rocky, rolling creek at a camp in North Georgia.

On the covered rocking-chair porch overlooking the rambunctious creek, alone, I cataloged my feelings. I felt chilly—it was March 12, so the weather was still cool. I also felt loved—my wife had provided me with food and snacks, had even made freshly baked chocolate chip cookies for me, and I had found a dozen or so little love notes stuck to my clothes in my suitcase. That all felt so good.

I also felt frazzled after a long, hard, nonstop day at work. My plans to leave early and take a leisurely drive two hours north of Atlanta were dashed when a last minute crash-and-burn project hit the ad agency where I worked. Even so, I left work late while others kept laboring into the night, so I felt guilty too.

I was also scared, unsettled. Even though I had made the trip to this campground several times, I got lost driving there in the dark. But now I was feeling safer. And a little hopeful, though I had no idea what I would do or what would happen. I was just going to play it by ear.

When I wrote my journal entry, I had just read "Evening Prayer" in *The Book of Common Prayer*, and found it moving and refreshing. Maybe this would work after all.

Saturday morning, after a restful night's sleep, I started with "Morning Prayer," another part of "praying the hours" in the liturgical tradition. In the rite's prayer of confession, the phrase "and what we have left undone" struck me. I was feeling as though my life was full of "left undones." A series of verses came to me as I read the prayer book:

> Oh yes, he's our God,
> and we're the people he pastures, the flock he feeds.
> Drop everything and listen, listen as he speaks. (Psalm 95:7)

> Oh! Teach us to live well!
> Teach us to live wisely and well! (Psalm 90:12)

> And let the loveliness of our Lord, our God, rest on us,
> confirming the work that we do.
> Oh, yes. Affirm the work that we do! (Psalm 90:17)

> "Anyone on God's side listens to God's words. This is why you're not listening—because you're not on God's side." (John 8:47)

As verse tumbled upon verse, I found myself weeping. Then I remember almost literally feeling the embrace of Jesus. My simple notes, hardly able to capture the depth of renewal I felt, read: "Overcome by the love and presence of Jesus! Weeping tears of love and joy—not sadness. Feel accepted and loved and cherished like a friend and lover."

Finally, another verse came to me:

> God can do anything, you know—far more than you could ever imagine or guess or request in your wildest dreams! He does it not by pushing us around but by working within us, his Spirit deeply and gently within us.
> Glory to God in the church!
> Glory to God in the Messiah, in Jesus!
> Glory down all the generations!
> Glory through all millennia! Oh, yes! (Ephesians 3:20-21)

This experience carried on through the rest of my retreat weekend, and helped me get started on a journey of opening my eyes to God's wider, more challenging will for me.

Two years later, during another Lent, I went on another private retreat. I was a week away from starting my job at The Protestant Hour, and I wanted to prepare myself by centering on God.

I wrote on March 8 of that year in my journal:

> *Here I am. Thursday morning in the McRaes' cottage. Gorgeous morning—but cold.*
>
> *Here I am. A week from today I will be Executive Producer of The Protestant Hour, Inc. The change will be traumatic, but I'm excited. So much to do. Overwhelming.*
>
> *Here I am. Kind of empty. Scared. Surfacey. I have kept busy here, maybe too busy.*
>
> *Here I am: Me! Oh, God, how I need you. Who do I think I am? Have I defrauded these people? Thank you, God, for bringing me to this place.*

Part of that retreat, and three more annual Lenten retreats after that one, involved another discipline: painting a Station of the Cross for our church's annual display. The many talented artists who attend our church every year select a particular station to paint.

I have found this exercise not only physically challenging, but also emotionally moving and faith-building. As I paint on a large canvas the image of Christ carrying the cross . . . or being stripped of his clothes . . . or dying on the cross, I can't help but feel pulled into the act, sensing how it felt, wondering how I would have responded, desiring Jesus' presence.

During such times I can get away from the dry routine of life and draw closer to Jesus, get away with him, and recover my life. I experience real rest in his presence, walking with him, working with him, seeing how he does things and trying to follow along. He restores me and energizes me, enabling me to return to my life with hope and renewed energy.

How about you? Do you need a rest? Jesus beckons generously to you: "Come to me."

Jesus, I want to keep company with you. I want to learn to live freely and lightly. I want to be able to sense your embrace not only on those too infrequent retreats, but here. Now. Today. Right in the midst of this routine life you have led me into. Amen. ■

23

COME CLOSER

... AND REMEMBER CHRIST'S SACRIFICE

> In the course of their meal, having taken and blessed the bread, he broke it and gave it to them. Then he said,
> "Take, this is my body." (Mark 14:22)

JESUS AND HIS CLOSEST friends, his most devoted followers, gathered to celebrate the Passover. This was the night they remembered the deliverance of the nation of Israel from Egypt, when the angel of death passed over them, giving them the opportunity to leave Egypt, the land of bondage.

With just a few simple words, Jesus transformed their perceptions.

The Book of Common Prayer summarizes the scene this way:

> On the night he was handed over to suffering and death,
> our Lord Jesus Christ took bread; and when he had given
> thanks to you, he broke it, and gave it to his disciples,
> and said, "Take, eat: This is my Body, which is given for
> you. Do this for the remembrance of me."[2]

As Jesus handed them the unleavened bread, he told them it was his body, and to take it and eat it.

In other words, make it yours.

Make it *you.*

When Jesus gave the disciples the cup of wine, he said it was his blood. Again, in *The Book of Common Prayer:*

> After supper he took the cup of wine; and when he had given thanks, he gave it to them, and said, "Drink this, all of you: This is my Blood of the new Covenant, which is shed for you and for many for the forgiveness of sins. Whenever you drink it, do this for the remembrance of me."[3]

They all drank from it. They tasted the sweetness and the bitterness, they inhaled the wine's musky aroma, the pungent bouquet. They experienced the warmth of it entering their inmost self.

His body, his blood: With you whenever you eat these simple staples of daily nourishment.

His body, his blood: In your presence whenever you gather in fellowship around his table.

His body, his blood: Alive. Within you. Nourishing you. Present with you always.

Jesus. Real. Alive. Present. Now.

Jesus warned his gathered friends in that upstairs room that the darkest day in earth's history was coming, tomorrow. But that he would be with them day in and day out, forever. All they had to do was remember. Every time they ate bread and drank wine they would be reminded of their beloved Lord's presence. Within them.

So can you.

Think back on all the communion services you've been part of. All those "routine" services. All the special ones at church retreats or intimate gatherings. Year after year of communion services.

Each one, time after time, is a reminder. A reminder to

remember Jesus. His presence within you. His fellowship around the table with you. His self-sacrificing love within and among you.

Take. Eat. Drink . . . and remember.

Jesus, I want to grab hold of you and never let go. Remind me of your constant presence, your sacrificial love, your eternal provision. Amen. ■

24

COME CLOSER

. . . AND PREPARE TO SEE GOD WORK

GOD said to Moses, "Go down. Warn the people not to break through the barricades to get a look at GOD lest many of them die. And the priests also, warn them to prepare themselves for the holy meeting, lest GOD break out against them." (Exodus 19:21-22)

GOD HAD BECKONED MOSES to come closer, to climb up the mountain. But then God met Moses halfway (see verse 20) and told him to go back down to make sure the people didn't attempt to get a look at the Holy One.

If you had been there and knew God was coming near, wouldn't you have wanted to do everything you could to catch a glimpse? Wouldn't the awesome spectacle have intrigued you?

Of course! But like a moth to a bug zapper, the results would have been devastating.

That's what happened when King David's servant, Uzzah, presuming to steady the holy ark of the covenant to keep it from falling as it was carried by wagon over rough roadways back to Jerusalem, reached out and touched it. God's holiness "broke out" and struck poor Uzzah down (see 2 Samuel 6:3-8).

Sinful human life cannot exist in the pure, perfect presence of almighty God, and the Israelites weren't ready to behold the sheer holy glory of the Lord of hosts. Even the priests, those set apart for God's service, had to go through intricate preparations of body, mind, and heart in order to approach God.

You see, coming close to God is serious business. Deadly serious. In our casual, easygoing cultural style, this fact doesn't jibe with our picture of God. We consider God to be our spiritual friend, father, or counselor—our invisible good buddy we can just hang out with. In many ways, through Christ, God is just that.

But in adopting that loose image, we lose sight of the almighty holiness of God—a holiness that requires cleansing and preparation before we can even think of entering into the presence.

Thanks be to God, in Christ we are forgiven and cleansed, set free from the sin that keeps us under the threat of holy horror. Because of Christ we are counted as righteous. Covered by Christ's righteousness, we become holy, as holy as God is. Even to the extent that God's Holy Spirit dwells within us.

Still, God can "break out" today—in us, through us—but in a much different way. It's not the unexpected zap of God's judgment of sin; it's the radical, magnanimous, overpowering outbreak of love. For us, and for others we come in contact with.

When we are in right relation with this powerfully holy God, we become a channel of that outbreak into a world that so desperately needs God's loving touch.

God's holy presence is within you, child of God. Don't keep it bottled up. Let it break out through you to those around you.

God, I am in desperate need of your holiness, your presence. Thank you for sanctifying me through Christ—for making me whole and holy. Use me as a channel for your regenerating presence to others today. Amen. ■

25

COME CLOSER

. . . AND JOIN THE CELEBRATION

"Come!" say the Spirit and the Bride.
Whoever hears, echo, "Come!"
Is anyone thirsty? Come!
All who will, come and drink,
Drink freely of the Water of Life! (Revelation 22:17)

THE SPIRIT OF GOD bids you to come.

The Bride—the beloved of Christ, the church throughout all time, the saints from every place—invites you to come.

And when you come, you are encouraged to turn around and tell others to join you.

You who are parched and dry, come to the Water of Life.
You who are empty and needy, come to fullness.
You who feel fraudulent and false, come to authenticity.
You who feel burdened and weary, come to rest.
You who are lost, come to discovery.
You who desire meaning and purpose, come to fulfillment.
You who seek truth and life, come to joy.
Come and drink deeply and freely and joyfully of the Water of Life.
This is the invitation of your life. Accept it, and it is yours eternally.
Come! Come and drink!

Gather around the fountain that will never run dry. The fountain of effervescent spirituality. The fountain of sweet surrender. The fountain of refreshing joy. The fountain of abundant living.

The party is just beginning. Don't be late.

God, I hear you calling me. I see you beckoning to me. Loosen the shackles of fear and uncertainty that keep me from coming to you. I am thirsty for you. I want to drink freely of the Water of Life. And live in your joy forever. Amen. ■

PART TWO

GOD INVITES YOU TO

LIVE ABUNDANTLY

26

LIVE ABUNDANTLY

. . . BY BELIEVING GOD IS AT WORK

When Jesus saw her, his heart broke. He said to her, "Don't cry." (Luke 7:13)

PICTURE THIS: JESUS, SURROUNDED by his twelve disciples and a large crowd trailing behind them, walks into the village of Nain.

The atmosphere hums with anticipation and joy. The word about this radical preacher and healer has been spreading like crabgrass on a summer lawn, and people are coming from all around to catch the show.

It's a parade, only without the marching bands. The crowd is chattering, wondering what would happen next. Will Jesus do something miraculous? Astonishing? Will he reveal a surprising truth? Challenge his followers?

On they walk, the aged and the children, men and women, believers and skeptics.

As they approach the village gates, this jubilant crowd runs right into another parade of a much different sort: a funeral procession.

A weeping mother leads a solemn line of mourners. A widow who is now childless faces a life of emptiness and poverty.

But as soon as Jesus sees her, his heart breaks. He knows the devastation she faces. Her loss is immeasurable. She has no husband, no son to provide for her in a culture that did little to provide for widows.

His words to her elicit a gasp from both crowds: "Don't cry."

Don't cry?

How can he say that? If anyone has a right to cry, it is this woman! She faces destitution and loneliness—and there is no way out.

Except with Jesus.

After Jesus tells the woman not to cry, he does something that stuns the crowd: "Then he went over and touched the coffin. The pallbearers stopped. He said, 'Young man, I tell you: Get up'" (verse 14).

Get up?

How can the dead get up?

First Jesus tells the woman to stop crying, and then he gives her a reason: "The dead son sat up and began talking. Jesus presented him to his mother" (verse 15).

In an instant, her situation is utterly changed, her hope restored. She is saved through the miraculous act of this stranger leading a motley parade of followers.

The gospel story tells us how the crowd reacted: "They all realized they were in a place of holy mystery, that God was at work among them. They were quietly worshipful—and then noisily grateful, calling out among themselves, 'God is back, looking to the needs of his people!'" (verse 16).

Suddenly, both sets of marchers—the curious and the mournful—are celebrating. The reality of what they have seen hits them like a nuclear blast at the core of their souls. They acknowledge the source of Christ's power and worship the holy mystery of God at work in their very presence by celebrating. Noisily. Gratefully.

God is back!

Now put yourself in the place of the mourning mother. You

have suffered a loss—a job, a friend, a spouse, a child, a dream. You feel unable to deal with the situation, empty of power and facing a hopeless future.

Jesus sees you. And tells you, "Don't cry." And then he gives you a reason not to.

Wouldn't you join the celebration of the faithful? Wouldn't you agree with the grateful, worshipful, noisy revelers that "God is back, looking to the needs of his people"?

It's true. Believe it. It's where abundant life begins.

Jesus, thank you for your revolutionary comfort. I celebrate your powerful care in my life. Thank you for seeing me, knowing me, loving me, accepting me. Help me do the same to others. Amen. ■

27

. . . BY TAKING RESPONSIBILITY FOR LIFE

> God blessed them: "Prosper! Reproduce! Fill Earth! Take charge!" (Genesis 1:28)

LIVING ABUNDANTLY INVOLVES ACKNOWLEDGING what may be a very surprising revelation:

God trusts you.

God speaks the same empowering words to you that he spoke to Adam and Eve: "Prosper! Reproduce! Fill Earth! Take charge!"

Go for it! Make life happen. Reproduce what's good and holy and true in you; spread it around to others. Fill the planet with righteousness and justice and holy truth. Exercise fruitful dominion.

Take charge!

God has gifted us with all the wisdom and resources and strength we need to fulfill this calling. The Bible says each of us was created to be "godlike, reflecting God's nature" (verse 27). Creativity, productivity, choice, and authority mark that nature.

But how do we "take charge"? Is God telling us to take things into our own hands and decide for ourselves what we are supposed to do? Unfortunately, this is a trap that many of us fall into, particularly when we have had some success or experience.

When I became the executive producer of The Protestant Hour, I sensed God's call to the position, but I really didn't have a clue as to what I was doing, so I had to depend on God for direction and guidance. I simply launched out, going for broke, approaching problems with fresh creativity, enthused by the potential of this ministry.

The first several months I was a tornado of energy: making changes to our radio program, pursuing new broadcast outlets, restoring neglected relationships with our participating denominations and associated organizations. But after a year or so, I started doing the same right, good things in my own strength instead of in God's. I began to function on autopilot.

Guess what happened. My strength ebbed away into exhaustion; my passion dwindled into negativity. So when harder times came for the organization, I had few resources to draw on and easily became discouraged.

Ever been there? More important, are you there today? Do you doubt whether you can do the job God has called you to do?

If so, remember that God has blessed you—has made you in the divine image and given you exactly what you need to follow your calling.

Next time you feel discouraged, lift your eyes to heaven. Realize God's invitation to abundant living means doing what you were made to do. Renew your trust in the God who urges and cheers you on. Drink deeply from the bottomless pool of divine wisdom and strength. Depend on God's power and strength to do the work. Let go of your own fears and fetters. Rely on all who have been called along with you.

God created you to make life happen—and trusts you to do just that.

God, I am overwhelmed by the responsibility you place on me, the trust you have in me to live abundantly and serve you in creative, effective ways. I accept your challenge. Give me the trust, wisdom, and vision I need to make it happen. For your glory. Amen. ■

28

LIVE ABUNDANTLY

. . . BY CONFRONTING YOUR SIN

GOD said to Joshua, "Get up. Why are you groveling?" (Joshua 7:10)

SUDDENLY, EVERYTHING WAS FALLING apart.

One sinful act by one person, Achan, threatened to undo all the progress Israel had made under Joshua in the land God was giving them. After Israel miraculously defeated Jericho, Achan pilfered some valuable contraband from the city—forbidden booty most likely related to idolatrous worship. That sinful act led to the shattering consequence of utter defeat at the hands of Ai.

The Israelites had confidently spied out the land and their plan of attack seemed sound. Only one problem: It didn't work.

The soldiers of Ai swarmed against the Israelites and struck them down, and Israel experienced defeat for the first time in their seemingly unstoppable quest for the Promised Land.

The setback shocked and devastated Joshua. He fell face to the ground before the ark of the Lord, weeping desperately before God for hours:

> Oh, oh, oh . . . Master, GOD. Why did you insist on bringing this people across the Jordan? To make us victims of the Amorites? To wipe us out? Why didn't we just settle

> down on the east side of the Jordan? Oh, Master, what can I say after this, after Israel has been run off by its enemies? When the Canaanites and all the others living here get wind of this, they'll gang up on us and make short work of us—and then how will you keep up *your* reputation? (verses 7-9)

Ever said something similar to God? Most of us have. One surprise attack, one single reversal, and we want to give up. We feel like throwing the whole bathtub out the window, baby, bathwater, and all. We writhe in self-absorbed agony, questioning God. We think, *How could God treat me like this? What happened to all those loving promises? Doesn't God realize what this will mean to me?*

God finally silenced Joshua's distress, saying, "Get up."

Stand up. Stop whining and groveling. Be strong in the face of this setback. Take responsibility for what has happened. Know that God is with you, but there are some things you must deal with.

Israel had sinned. Yes, just one man had actually sinned, but the Israelites were one people, one family. The sinful act of one darkened the face of all: "They've broken the covenant I commanded them; they've taken forbidden plunder—stolen and then covered up the theft, squirreling it away with their own stuff" (verse 11).

You see, a covenant works both ways. God's promises are fulfilled in obedient hearts.

Thankfully, sin-darkened hearts can be made new again. God instructed Joshua, "So get started. Purify the people. Tell them: Get ready for tomorrow by purifying yourselves" (verse 13).

Of course, not all setbacks are the consequence of sin. But all sin has consequences. When you, like Joshua, find yourself suffering over a loss or a setback caused by sin—yours or someone else's—

and questioning God's goodness and doubting God's loving promises, remember to stand up and take responsibility for what you have done. Get clean if you need to. Make things right if necessary. And then get back to it.

Abundant hearts are clean hearts.

God, help me to see your hand behind the circumstances of my life. If I need to deal with sin and separation from you, help me to do that. If I need to stand up and move on, give me the strength to do that. Amen. ■

29

LIVE ABUNDANTLY

. . . BY FOLLOWING JESUS

Passing along the beach of Lake Galilee, he saw Simon and his brother Andrew net-fishing. Fishing was their regular work. Jesus said to them, "Come with me. I'll make a new kind of fisherman out of you. I'll show you how to catch men and women instead of perch and bass." They didn't ask questions. They dropped their nets and followed. (Mark 1:16-18)

JESUS MAY HAVE LOOKED like an ordinary beachcomber, walking leisurely along the shoreline. But he had important matters on his mind. He had some choices to make that would shape the effectiveness of his work on earth.

Whom should he ask to join him? Who should walk with him, learn from him, risk with him? Whom should he ask to sacrifice their everyday existences in order to enter a world that required absolute trust in God?

Whom should Jesus choose? And who would choose to follow?

He was walking and praying and thinking when he saw two men fishing. They were hard, leathery men, beefy and salty. Their eyes squinted, forming spider webs of wrinkles, due to the sunlight dancing off the Sea of Galilee. Their hands were worn, calloused, cracked, and thick from their work—tough, smelly work that paid a living wage and kept their existence stable.

Jesus approached these two men with a challenge, an invitation to more: "Come with me. I'll make a new kind of fisherman out of you. I'll show you how to catch men and women instead of perch and bass."

They dropped their nets immediately; they didn't even think it over.

They just followed Jesus.

Did they know what they were doing? Were they so burned out with fishing that they jumped at the first invitation to something new and different? Were they so dissatisfied with the way things were going, with life's frustrations and fears, that they leapt at the chance to stretch their boundaries?

We don't know exactly why they followed this unusual teacher, we just know they did. Certainly Jesus cut a compelling figure. His teachings were bold and gripping. Apparently, Peter and Andrew had already encountered Jesus once (see John 1:35-42).

The reason that they followed him is not as important as the fact that they did. They listened to his invitation and they accepted it. They put aside the nets that tangled their lives, took that first step, and followed.

They were ordinary people, living their lives as best they could, but apparently wanting something more in life—something meaningful and purposeful and real.

What about you? Will you, too, hear the invitation and follow—wherever Jesus leads you?

Jesus, the people you called were just ordinary people. Like me. But you gave them an extraordinary challenge to follow you. It's the same challenge you give me today. Help me desire to respond to your invitation. Amen. ■

30

LIVE ABUNDANTLY

. . . BY LETTING JESUS LEAD

> Calling the crowd to join his disciples, he said, "Anyone who intends to come with me has to let me lead. You're not in the driver's seat; *I* am. Don't run from suffering; embrace it. Follow me and I'll show you how." (Mark 8:34)

JESUS' WORDS FLY IN the face of everything our culture tells us.

Aren't we supposed to be leaders? Don't we have to take destiny into our hands and charge forward?

Aren't we supposed to take control of our lives? Live it as we think best?

Aren't we supposed to soothe our hurts and deal with our wounds so as to get rid of them? Don't we choose to avoid suffering and pain and conflict and difficulties?

Don't we deserve the best? Haven't we earned success and wealth and position and power? Don't we have the right to claim whatever we feel we need from God?

According to Jesus, we have to let him lead. Let him be in control. Let him run things his way. This instruction is for all his followers—not just his disciples, not just his closest friends, not just the religious leaders, pastors, professionals. For everybody.

Let Jesus lead, and he might just lead you to the cross. But, he says, don't hesitate. Don't avoid it. Embrace it.

What does this mean in the life of garden-variety followers like you and me? Are we really going to get killed because of our faith?

Probably not. But, when we seek to bring Jesus' loving justice into this world, we might run into all sorts of opposition. We might be shunned. We might even lose a few "friends."

Some time ago just before the war in Iraq began, the *Day 1* radio program featured a well-known preacher, one of our listeners' favorites, who encouraged each of us and our nation as a whole to take a hard look at our self-assumed right to be in charge. Drawing a parallel between Naaman, the mighty warrior who sought to be healed of his leprosy by the prophet Elisha, and our country, she urged us to assume an attitude of humility, to listen to our neighbors around the world, to seek to obey God's commands even when they make little sense.

We had an unusually high number of requests for sermon transcripts that week—the message struck a deep chord in most listeners. On the other hand, we also received a couple of strident phone calls from good Christians excoriating us for our anti-Americanism. One man called a half dozen times to curse at us for daring to question America's status as the leader of the world.

He may have missed the point of the message, but his reaction demonstrates how much most of us—on both a personal and a national level—prefer to be in charge, on top and in control. We don't naturally embrace the path Jesus took, the path of humility, justice, and suffering.

No, humility isn't something we naturally want to do. It may not even be the American way. But it is Jesus' way. It's the way of life Jesus wants us to embrace. Even if the results are painful.

By the way—that man who called half a dozen times to rail against our program? His final call was one of humble apology. His pastor had encouraged him to settle down and realize that our intentions were honorable, and that while we might disagree on some major issues, we are still brothers in the faith.

That's a beautiful example of letting Jesus lead.

Jesus, sometimes I think I try too hard to understand what it means to follow you. I spend so much time trying to make sense of it that I never get around to actually doing it. You carried a cross for a purpose. You have a cross for me to carry. You call me to put my own needs and desires and interests behind your own and follow your example into the unknown. It feels very big. Yet it also feels very simple. It's what I want to do. Help me do it. Amen. ■

31

LIVE ABUNDANTLY

. . . BY FILLING UP WITH JOY

> Don't drink too much wine. That cheapens your life. Drink the Spirit of God, huge draughts of him. Sing hymns instead of drinking songs! Sing songs from your heart to Christ. Sing praises over everything, any excuse for a song to God the Father in the name of our Master, Jesus Christ. (Ephesians 5:18-20)

ONE DAY LAST WEEK (actually it could be just about any day of any week), I was driving in achingly slow Atlanta traffic during the morning rush hour, weighed down by concerns and fears, and grumbling in disappointment and discouragement.

What should I do about that disgruntled listener to our radio program? When will we receive that major gift we'd been promised? How would I make the new budget balance? And what about the people close to me who were going through such a tough time? And why hadn't my friend called me for lunch like he'd promised? And why is that idiot driving so close to my rear bumper?

Then, on the back of a car in front of me in the next lane, I saw the stylized descending dove, the well-known symbol of Spirit-filled believers. I'd seen that symbol probably dozens of times in my life, but this particular morning it jarred my negative thought patterns to a halt.

Then God's Spirit brought to mind this verse from Ephesians, and in an act of faith, I popped a praise CD into the player. A few minutes later, I had set aside my worries and found myself singing at the top of my lungs. If you'd have seen me, you might well have thought I was drunk!

By the time I arrived at my office a half hour or so later, I felt disappointed to have to leave my mobile sanctuary. But I was able to take this spirit of singing with me throughout the day.

What had caused my emotional aboutface?

My choice to "drink the Spirit of God," to "sing praises."

Praise lifts the spirit. Sends it soaring. Fills us with joy. That's why God beckons us to fill ourselves to overflowing with holy joy, instead of getting drunk on wine or some other cheap substitute for joy, such as drugs, food, or other addictive substances or practices. God knows that none of these will satisfy us. At best, they can only make us feel better temporarily.

How can you "get drunk" on God? By opening your heart, mind, and spirit, and intentionally seeking God's presence through prayer and meditation. By yearning for God's cool, clean, rejuvenating spiritual refreshment.

This joyful filling up on the Spirit of God isn't meant to be a one-time event. God intends for it to be an ongoing, intentional action. No matter where you are, no matter what you're doing, God invites you to "*Sing praises over everything, any excuse for a song to God the Father in the name of our Master, Jesus Christ.*"

Drink up! And sing heartily.

God, I yearn to be filled with your presence, your power, your purpose, your joy. Always. Let me hear the music of eternity in my soul and empower me to sing along with everything I've got. Amen. ■

. . . BY LIVING A HOLY LIFE

So roll up your sleeves, put your mind in gear, be totally ready to receive the gift that's coming when Jesus arrives. Don't lazily slip back into those old grooves of evil, doing just what you feel like doing. You didn't know any better then; you do now. As obedient children, let yourselves be pulled into a way of life shaped by God's life, a life energetic and blazing with holiness. God said, "I am holy; you be holy." (1 Peter 1:13-16)

THE APOSTLE PETER WROTE this letter to believers who faced dark, terrible days of persecution. Many had lost their jobs, their friends, their homes, and their possessions. And many would lose their lives. Peter wanted to give them encouragement and instruction. So much was on the line. It was make or break time.

Peter knew that these believers could easily slide back into the safety and security of the culture around them, so he urged them to an obedient life, to a "*way of life shaped by God's life, a life energetic and blazing with holiness.*"

Even though we live in a different time and place, and may face different threats, we too need to hear this invitation to holiness. The lure of our society can be so subtle. Before we realize it, we fall back into old habits. We start pursuing wealth or fame or friends or good feelings. We let our spiritual practices slide. We get disconnected from the true, pure, holy power of God. We ignore the calling of our Savior on our lives.

Suddenly, the culture has swallowed us up again, and we don't realize it because we feel secure in its dark and hideous emptiness. After all, it's what we came out of. It's familiar. Comfortable. And so many others are there with us.

"Roll up your sleeves," God urges. "Put your mind in gear."

Make it your goal to live "a life energetic and blazing with holiness."

Being holy doesn't mean being better than other people or being exclusively right or specially blessed. It doesn't mean floating blissfully through the world with your mind in the heavenly clouds.

Being holy means being set apart—by God, for God. It means being prepared and useful for God's purposes. Shining with the light of redemption and righteousness. It means being made clean through the presence of the Holy Spirit—our sins and failures removed and replaced by the power and potential of God. Energized by the love of God. Devoted to the will of God.

Holiness isn't a feeling, it's a place. A place where God is. A place God wants you to be too. Make it your goal to live like this—"energetic and blazing with holiness."

Do you feel a bit inadequate? Slightly fraudulent? Totally incapable?

Don't worry. You are right where you need to be because that means you know you can't be holy on your own. You are ready for God to use you.

God, I plead for your holy energy, your holy light blazing within me and through me. Peel away the dark scabs of sin that keep that from happening. Cleanse me and sharpen me and shape me into the way of life shaped by God's life. Then use me for God's glory. Amen. ■

PATIENT INSTRUCTIONS

Mark 8:34

"Anyone who intends to come with me has to let me lead. You're not in the driver's seat; I am. Don't run from suffering; embrace it. Follow me + I'll show you how."

33

. . . BY LETTING THE WORD DWELL IN YOU

> Let the Word of Christ—the Message—have the run of the house. Give it plenty of room in your lives. Instruct and direct one another using good common sense. And sing, sing your hearts out to God! Let every detail in your lives—words, actions, whatever—be done in the name of the Master, Jesus, thanking God the Father every step of the way.
> (Colossians 3:16-17)

IMAGINE WHAT WOULD HAPPEN if you gave God's Word plenty of room in your soul, letting his Spirit run loose within you, with no hesitation, no holding back, no fear about what might happen if you lost control.

You might discover a mutual support system with your brothers and sisters, instructing and directing each other in the spirit of love and truth and mercy.

You might unleash a stream of common sense for living and start making choices with God's big picture in mind instead of reacting out of fear or selfishness.

You might find your heart lifted, singing and soaring in praise as a matter of routine.

You might live out every detail of your life, conscious of the Master's beckoning to you, intentionally seeking to follow Christ wherever he might lead you.

You might take every step, live every moment, every day with a heart full of thanks for the heavenly God who provides your every need and promises you an eternity filled with lavish love and praise.

You might live in harmony with God and with one another.

You might live more abundantly.

Do you sense the gracious invitation to let the Word of Christ dwell within you, starting right now?

Isn't it an invitation worth accepting?

God, your Word is life. Fill my heart and soul with it, let it fill me to overflowing. Let it have its way with me. Let me walk in obedience and love with eternal thanks. Amen. ■

LIVE ABUNDANTLY

. . . BY IMMERSING YOURSELF IN SCRIPTURE

> And don't for a minute let this Book of The Revelation be out of mind. Ponder and meditate on it day and night, making sure you practice everything written in it. Then you'll get where you're going; then you'll succeed. (Joshua 1:8)

I LOVE BOOKS. EVERYTHING from Kierkegaard to Jack Kirby, from devotionals to dime novels.

Surrounding my easy chair are stacks of books, my "to-read" pile. At the present moment I'm reading books by Brennan Manning, Walt Wangerin, Henri Nouwen, Max Lucado, Madeleine L'Engle, Jacques Barzun, and Kahlil Gibran, among several others. I plan on reading a Celtic Christian prayerbook, a book on icons, Stephen King's book *On Writing*, and a collection of Flash Gordon Sunday newspaper comic strips by Mac Raboy.

By my bedside is the P. D. James novel I just finished and a Van Reid novel I'm about to begin, plus a reprint collection of the first Batman stories ever published. And in my bathroom (yes, I'm a bathroom reader too) are the latest issues of *The Week, Christian History,* and *Scottish Life*.

On my Palm PDA I have digitized versions of *Ben Hur, The Brothers Karamazov, Great Expectations*, St. John of the Cross's *Dark Night of the Soul, The Book of Common Prayer,* and several others.

In my closet is a box containing a manuscript of over a thousand pages, which was one of the most sublime reading experiences of my life: It's Michael Chabon's first draft of the Pulitzer-prize-winning novel, *The Amazing Adventures of Kavalier & Clay,* which he graciously asked me to read.

I am a reader, always immersed in about three or four or more books at a time. But when I read God's invitation to Joshua to ponder and meditate on Scripture, I have to question my reading priorities.

I am immersed in reading, but am I immersed in God's Word? Am I intentional about making Scripture part of my daily reading routine? Do I think about it, meditate on it, roll it over in my mind and heart and soul? Knock it around, kick its tires, study it in the light of the sun, throw it against the wall and see if it sticks?

God tells Joshua that, if he's going to succeed in his efforts to subdue the Promised Land for Israel, he can't let God's Word out of his mind for a moment.

So, God also invites us to consider Scripture. Ponder it. Meditate on it. Be intentional about it. Keep it front and center in our conscious thinking.

But don't stop there. God invites us to meditate on the Word so that we might *do* the Word. Live it out, follow it, make it part of our being. For that to happen requires that we be immersed in it. Saturated by it. Soaking it in.

And that requires time and effort.

Are your reading priorities in good order? Have you put first things first? Do you allow yourself sufficient time in your waking hours to think about what God is calling you to do, what God is challenging you to be about?

The abundant life that God invites us to includes being intentional about spending time meditating on the Scriptures, wrestling with what you hear, questioning and probing and considering and thinking through God's Word in the indwelling presence of the Spirit.

That's how to "get where you're going" today.

God, impress upon me the need to be intentional about reading, knowing, and doing your Word. Guide me through my study; make it real, alive, engaging, effective. Amen. ■

35

. . . BY EMBRACING GOD'S CALL

GOD told Abram: "Leave your country, your family, and your father's home for a land that I will show you." (Genesis 12:1)

THERE COMES A TIME when each of us who accepts God's invitation to abundant living must leave home, comfort, familiarity, and security to step out into an unknown land—the future God has for us.

For me that time was Memorial Day weekend in 1976. On my way to spend the weekend with my folks on the James River in Virginia, I side-tripped through Richwood, in the eastern mountains of West Virginia, to touch base before being added to the payroll of *The West Virginia Hillbilly,* a weekly newspaper edited and published by one of the state's most beloved eccentrics, Jim Comstock.

I discovered that Richwood was a postcard vision—a beautiful little one-stoplight town that filled the Cherry River Valley, surrounded by lush wooded hills. My heart beat with nervous anticipation as I drove into the heart of town.

I found the rickety, white frame Palotta Building smack in the middle of town, right next to a busy Union 76 gas station. At the time, this modest, ancient structure was the *Hillbilly* World Headquarters. Downstairs was a bookstore crammed with books by, for, and about West Virginians, some of them published by

Comstock himself. Upstairs was a suite of offices, most of them filled completely, floor to ceiling, with books and papers. Overlooking Main Street and stretching across the front of the building was Jim's ephemera-strewn office.

I spent maybe a half-hour getting the nickel tour of the building and chatting with Jim about getting started after the holiday. He graciously offered to let me live in an apartment. Right on the premises. Free.

He took me upstairs to show it to me. "This will be your room," he announced proudly. "You can live here," he added, as though trying to convince me he was telling the truth.

What I saw stunned me. Books, boxes, papers, and assorted odds and ends filled the tiny room from floor to ceiling. It had a window, but the view was the wall of the building next door. Just behind this ten-by-twelve foot room was a bathroom. I could tell because I could see the claw feet of an old bathtub underneath a mound of junk.

I smiled weakly. Sensing my chagrin, Comstock quickly assured me, "We're going to clean this out and paint it and get a couch in here for you to sleep on. It'll be ready by the time you get back on Monday."

Okay. Sure.

This was Thursday.

I soon left, wondering what in the world I was getting myself into. I tried to forget my doubts that weekend and enjoyed the time with my family in Virginia. But my heart was full of concern on the drive back that next Monday.

Sure enough, that little room had been transformed. It was clean, painted, furnished. I was impressed.

That room would be my home for nearly a year. There was only one problem with it: It was right next door to Jim's office. He came in every morning about six and turned on the TV. Loud. And started to work on his manual typewriter, which sounded like a machine gun.

That generally woke me up. So I'd take a bath in that classy old tub, dress, and report for duty, with no idea where I might end up that night.

"Pete!" he'd bark in an energetic, high-pitched voice, "Here's what I want you to do today."

And I'd be off on another adventure. Covering a coal miners' march in Washington, D.C., or overseeing the printing of a special two-hundred-page newspaper issue celebrating the nation's Bicentennial. Selling ad space to some very dubious businessmen or taking Jim's place as grand marshal in a small-town parade. Giving a speech at a Pearl Buck Birthplace Chautauqua or typesetting some headlines and pasting up some pages. Covering the state legislature session or interviewing the just-elected governor. Investigating old railroad ghost towns or chauffeuring Jim to a speaking engagement while he wrote his lively editorials on a yellow legal pad.

During that period of my life I questioned what I—and God—was doing. But looking back I can see how much I learned and how foundational that experience was for much of what I would do later in life.

What if I hadn't taken that terrifying step? What if I hadn't listened to God's inward call? I would have lost a lifetime of wonderful memories packed into those three-plus years.

I'm certainly no Abram, but I do hope to be a willing child of God, sensitive to divine coaxing, open to God's calling for me—no matter my age or how overwhelming, strange, and faraway it might appear.

How about you?

God, make me sensitive to your calling on my life, responsive to your beckoning to me moment by moment. Like Abram, I want to heed the call without hesitation, because my trust in you is solid and ever-growing. Amen. ■

36

. . . BY FOLLOWING GOD WHOLEHEARTEDLY

"Give it everything you have, heart and soul. Make sure you carry out The Revelation that Moses commanded you, every bit of it. Don't get off track, either left or right, so as to make sure you get to where you're going." (Joshua 1:7)

MOSES HAD ACCOMPLISHED THE impossible-made-inevitable. He had led the large, boisterous, doubting, needy nation of Israel out of their Egyptian captivity and through the punishing wilderness for forty years.

Now this nation of hundreds of thousands stood on the brink of a new life. Finally, the Promised Land lay before them. But Moses was no longer their leader. Joshua was.

Imagine having to follow someone like Moses. What was going through Joshua's head when God gave him his marching orders? "Strength! Courage! You are going to lead this people to inherit the land that I promised to give their ancestors" (verse 6).

Crossing the Jordan River and entering the already occupied land would certainly be no simple exercise, yet God placed this weighty responsibility on Joshua's shoulders. It would require incredible administrative ability. Limitless trust in God. The inner resources to handle the incomprehensible needs of so many people.

How must Joshua have felt?

Sure, he had boldly declared the job as doable—but that was

before he knew he would be the one God chose to do the job. Did he ever regret his boldness? Did he wonder if he had spoken too soon?

We don't know. The Bible doesn't say. But we do know that God chose Joshua, as God had chosen Moses. God's word to Joshua was simple and clear: Be strong. Be courageous. "Give it everything you have, heart and soul."

Give it everything you have. A funny thing happens when we give everything we have to fulfilling our life purpose. We discover resources and abilities within that we never knew we possessed. We experience a creative energy we never tapped into before.

Not only did God tell Joshua to give heart and soul to entering and subduing the land, God also told him to obey the commandments given to Moses, beginning with the command to trust God, to put God first in all that he did. No matter how Joshua felt about what God was calling him to do, he had to trust that God would not have given him a goal without also giving him all the skill, insight, and inner resources to do the job.

Surely such knowledge would sustain and empower him during those times when he felt exhausted, stymied, discouraged, and frustrated beyond anything he'd ever known—which he surely felt, considering the enormity of the task.

We should never assume that just because God has called us to live abundantly we'll find life easy and pain-free. Yet, the guaranteed result of pure, wholehearted, courageous obedience is that we will get to where we're going—and we will experience joy in the journey. Because we are giving it all we've got, heart and soul.

God, you've set a calling before me. I want to give it everything I've got, heart and soul. Ease my fears and doubts by building my faith in you. Amen. ■

37

LIVE ABUNDANTLY

. . . BY GIVING JESUS YOUR HEART

> As he went out into the street, a man came running up, greeted him with great reverence, and asked, "Good Teacher, what must I do to get eternal life?" . . .
>
> Jesus looked him hard in the eye—and loved him! He said, "There's one thing left: Go sell whatever you own and give it to the poor. All your wealth will then be heavenly wealth. And come follow me." (Mark 10:17,21)

HE SEEMED A WELL-meaning guy.

He approached Jesus enthusiastically. He treated Jesus reverently, acknowledging him as a respected teacher. He clearly sought to know how to enter into an eternal relationship with God. He even knew his Scriptures.

He told Jesus he had followed the basic requirements of the faith—the Ten Commandments—since he was a boy (see verses 19-20). He hadn't killed anyone, didn't commit adultery, or steal, or lie, or cheat, and he honored his father and mother.

Check, check, check, check, check, and check.

Any of us would have taken a good look at this earnest young man and seen a success in the making. He had it all together. He lived the righteous life. He sought the truth.

But Jesus looked right through him, down into his very soul. What he saw caused a mixture of deep love and sorrow within the

Lord. He must have seen that a significant part of this young man wanted to be a sincere, dedicated follower of Christ. He might have been one of the most effective disciples ever. His winsomeness, his eager desire to learn, his willingness to follow—Jesus saw it and loved the man. His heart was good.

But it was not a fully open heart, ready to be given over to Jesus. Something held this man back, and Jesus saw it. Something that would continually trip the man up from following Christ fully and without hesitation, from living honestly and fully for God.

Yes, he was doing most everything right. But Jesus said, "There's one thing left: Go sell whatever you own and give it to the poor. All your wealth will then be heavenly wealth. And come follow me."

Jesus wanted this man's companionship. He wanted this man to follow him. But he also knew that this one thing would be an insurmountable obstacle for him. For the young man was too dependent upon his wealth and his possessions to be dependent upon Jesus.

"The man's face clouded over. This was the last thing he expected to hear, and he walked off with a heavy heart. He was holding on tight to a lot of things, and not about to let go" (verse 22).

Jesus drives a hard bargain. He expects a fully devoted heart. His love is a demanding love. A jealous love.

But when his love is accepted, it can bring freedom and heavenly wealth and lead us on a journey of incredible joy and fulfillment.

What's holding you back? Fear, uncertainty, selfishness? Some unhealthy relationships? The allure of pleasure, or possessions, or position, or power? What's keeping you from returning this limitless love of Christ for you?

Think those questions through. You have a choice to make.

Jesus, I admit to being a lot like this wealthy young man. It's so hard to let go of the things that I think bring me security and fulfillment and joy. It's so hard to love you back with no fetters, no stumbling blocks, nothing to hold me back from following you with utter freedom and trust. I see you look at me with eyes of love, wanting me to come follow you. Help me to keep my eyes locked on yours, and not look back. Amen. ■

38

LIVE ABUNDANTLY

. . . BY LETTING JESUS STRENGTHEN YOUR FAITH

> Jesus was abrupt: "Clear out! This girl isn't dead. She's sleeping." They told him he didn't know what he was talking about. (Matthew 9:24)

THE PEOPLE GATHERED AROUND Jairus's daughter thought Jesus was nuts. They even laughed at him! They were completely surprised by his nonsensical assertion. After all, the doctor had pronounced her dead! Did he think they were crazy?

Even though we know the rest of the story, can't we identify with them a little bit?

How often have we read something Jesus said and thought, *That doesn't apply to me. After all*, we rationalize, *today's world and culture are so different than when Jesus walked the earth. I have to take those differences into account before I believe or do or say something ridiculous. People might talk! In fact, they might think I'm nuts if I thought the way he thought or did what he encourages me to do. Right?*

If Jairus had dismissed Jesus' words, he would have missed out on the miracle of his daughter's resurrection. And that makes me wonder:

How often do we miss out on the miracle Jesus wants to share with us?

How often do we walk away from a trying, tough situation,

convinced it's hopeless, before inviting Jesus into it?

How often do we simply laugh at the proposition the Spirit brings to our heart because, well, it's just impossible?

How strong is our faith—really?

Jesus says to you and to me, "*Clear out!* Your thinking is upside down and backward. Your assumptions are dead—dead wrong! Your understanding is faulty, colored by your own misperceptions, fears, and doubts. Your faith is empty and powerless because you're so busy mourning over what you *think* reality is that you miss the *true* reality—that God can break in and transform the situation. That God can bring life out of death."

"But when Jesus had gotten rid of the crowd, he went in, took the girl's hand, and pulled her to her feet—alive" (verse 25).

If you want more faith, ask yourself:

- What situations in my life would Jesus confront?
- In what areas is my faith faulty or nonexistent?
- What doubts are keeping me powerless?
- What false assumptions are preventing me from experiencing God's powerful, surprising, and life-giving will?

Clear your mind of these things and your faith will grow stronger. You may be surprised at what God does as a result.

Jesus, open my eyes to my doubt and unbelief in your power to transform. Let me see the areas of my relationship with you that you yearn to bring to life. And help me open myself fully to life-giving faith in you. Amen. ■

39

LIVE ABUNDANTLY

. . . BY CHOOSING TO LOVE

> So, chosen by God for this new life of love, dress in the wardrobe God picked out for you: compassion, kindness, humility, quiet strength, discipline. . . . And regardless of what else you put on, wear love. It's your basic, all-purpose garment. Never be without it. (Colossians 3:12,14)

I WAS IN NEED of a wardrobe makeover.

For eleven years I'd been working at an advertising agency where we observed "casual Friday" every day of the week. Then I found myself in a new position that required a professional appearance every day. I had just two or three suits that fit me—almost.

I shared my quandary one Saturday morning with my friend Ruben. "Oh, I can help you there," he said. "I've got something like two dozen nice, tailored suits my boss gave me—he's worn them a few times and just keeps buying new ones. I've never even worn them. I'll be glad to give you some of those. They should fit you pretty well."

I looked at him in disbelief. He would give me some suits? Really expensive ones?

Turns out he never had the suits altered to fit him. Not only that, but Ruben gave me a handful of nearly new ties he never wore. His own workplace was becoming more dress-casual, so he rarely wore suits and ties anymore anyway.

Ruben provided me with several thousand dollars' worth of quality menswear. Those suits fit me to an absolute T—no alteration required.

Ruben did for me in a physical sense what God does for us in a spiritual sense. God has picked out a wonderful and priceless wardrobe for each of us. But they aren't designer label suits. They are worth far more.

The wardrobe God has given us includes *compassion, kindness, humility, quiet strength,* and *discipline.* Living abundantly requires putting on those traits, those character qualities, like a garment, so that they cover us from head to toe. We must clothe ourselves with one spiritual garment in particular: Love.

So each morning as I get dressed, thinking about the day ahead and its many and varied tasks and responsibilities, I try to keep this imperative in mind. As I pull on my pants, button my shirt, tie my tie, and put on my coat, I imagine myself putting on compassion, kindness, humility, quiet strength, discipline, and love.

Your life, your words, your actions are to exude those qualities with everyone you meet. It's as if the Holy Spirit dwelling within you permeates through your skin into the world around you, touching all you come in contact with.

You don't need to go out into the world naked. God has provided an exquisite wardrobe chosen expressly for you. Dress well.

God, clothe me, cover me so that all those I meet today will sense your presence, receive your compassion and kindness, and know your love. Amen. ■

40

. . . BY LOVING DEEPLY

> Love from the center of who you are; don't fake it. . . . Be good friends who love deeply; practice playing second fiddle. (Romans 12:9-10)

YEARS AGO, I JOINED an Internet discussion group regarding men's issues. One of the posts resonated with me. I don't even remember the specifics now, but the man who wrote it was clearly a person of faith.

As it turned out, the discussion group was so active I couldn't keep up with all the e-mails, so I dropped out after only a few days. But that one particular message kept echoing within me. So, boldly, I sent a note to its writer to share my thoughts about the points he'd raised.

At first he was a bit suspicious—not a bad trait when it comes to dealing with people on the Internet. But soon we were corresponding back and forth with regularity. His name was Jim, and he was an Episcopal priest in New York City. Very early on Jim also introduced me to another of his regular e-mail correspondents, a Methodist minister in South Africa named Colin.

Nearly ten years later, the three of us still correspond by e-mail at least once a week.

The richness of our Internet fellowship has been one of the joys of my life. Over the years we three have been able to share the deepest of pains and the greatest of joys. Colin and Jim are both a few years older than I am and have survived stints on the front lines of life and ministry, so I covet their hard-won wisdom and the perspective about life they bring to our discussions.

After a couple of years of online correspondence, Jim and I arranged to meet at his home in Queens. I'd never been to New York City before and was excited about the prospects. That weekend we first met in "real life," it seemed as though we'd known each other for years.

Jim was serving a parish in an area that had become predominantly Latino. So he and his wife, June, learned Spanish; ultimately the 11:00 A.M. service at his church became the Spanish-language service, while the 9:00 A.M. service met the needs of the old-line families who remained faithful to the church. I attended both services the weekend I first visited—and they were as different as night and day. One more traditional, the other much more lively, yet God's presence—and love—marked both of them.

A wonderful host, Jim took me around the city on that first visit to see many of the sites, making me feel so at home in the huge, strange city. We talked for hours about our faith, doubts, growing edges, hopes, families, and friends.

Jim epitomizes generosity of spirit, lavish affection, guileless wisdom, and comfortable presence. He is a "good friend who loves deeply." So are June and Colin and many other of my friends and loved ones who put their faith boldly into action.

All of them have discovered how to live like Jesus. All of them "love from the center" of who they are. All of them inspire me to join them in living the radically loving life of God.

God invites you and me to be this kind of person: active, energetic, giving, loving, and real. It's the only way to live. Will you join me in trying to live this way? In living and loving abundantly?

God, being the kind of person you call me to be requires putting my little fears, my selfish habits, my self-centered ways, my false masks aside and being real, loving deeply from my center with the love you have lavished on me. This is what I want. This is what I choose. Amen. ■

41

. . . BY LIVING PASSIONATELY

"Love the Lord your God with all your passion and prayer and muscle and intelligence—and that you love your neighbor as well as you do yourself."

"Good answer!" said Jesus. "Do it and you'll live."
(Luke 10:27-28)

SEVERAL YEARS AGO, TO commemorate our twentieth wedding anniversary, my wife wonderfully surprised me by giving me a trip to Scotland.

Our close friends were traveling to Edinburgh for a week for their honeymoon. Bonnie had figured out an ingenious way for us to meet them for the last couple of days of their honeymoon (yes, they agreed to this). After they returned home, we would stay another five days.

This was a dream come true for me. I've always been intrigued by Scotland, whose national hero is William Wallace. Surely I am a descendant!—even though he had no known children. At any rate, my family had always claimed Scotland as our homeland: Only later did I learn I had a Scots ancestor named Peter Wallace who sailed to America in the eighteenth century.

When the day in early September arrived, I could hardly contain myself. Our trans-Atlantic flight was, thankfully, uneventful (despite the fact that we were surrounded in coach by traveling Alvin Ailey dance troupers).

Even though Bonnie and I really hadn't slept in twenty-four

hours, we hit the Scottish ground running. We met our friends at the airport, went to check in at the hotel, and then immediately set off on foot toward Edinburgh's city center, taking it all in.

My mouth was agape. That entire week, as we traveled from Edinburgh's Royal Mile to St. Andrews to Stirling to Crail to the Trossachs to Caithness and elsewhere, I simply couldn't get enough of the sights and sounds and smells and tastes (even haggis!). I breathed it all in. I wanted every moment to last an hour; I wanted to grab every memory and hold on to it forever.

Bonnie said she had never seen me more engaged and energized. Everything seemed realer than real. I felt vibrant, expectant, full of life.

When we returned home, I eventually receded into my protective shell of routine busyness. But I wondered, *Why can't I live this passionately all the time? Why can't I approach my relationship with God* "with all [my] passion and prayer and muscle and intelligence"—*the way I approached the day's touring in Scotland? Why can't I relate to my world, my family, my work, my ministry, with all that fresh enthusiasm and interaction?*

And, by the way, why can't you?

A religious scholar once asked Jesus what he had to do to live eternally. At Jesus' prompting, he summarized God's law simply: Love God with everything you have, and love your neighbor as you do yourself.

It was the correct answer. Only one more thing, Jesus said: "Do it." Do it today—live and love God passionately with all that you are.

Jesus, I want to love with everything I've got. I want to live. Fully. Completely. With nothing holding me back. I want to be yours wholly, unstoppably. Show me how. Amen. ■

42

. . . BY PURSUING GOD

That means you must not give sin a vote in the way you conduct your lives. Don't give it the time of day. Don't even run little errands that are connected with that old way of life. Throw yourselves wholeheartedly and full-time—remember, you've been raised from the dead!—into God's way of doing things. (Romans 6:12-13)

I HAD A FRIEND in college who was active in the same Christian organization that I participated in. It was a growing, supportive community of students that met in small groups throughout the week. My friend spent large amounts of time in his dorm room reading the Bible and agonizing over past faults, ways he'd hurt people, and a few colorful sins he'd committed in his youth.

With a goal to make amends and move on, this can be a good thing to do. But my friend kept focusing on past sins week after week, and several of us became concerned about him. Anytime any of us would invite him to catch a movie or go to a basketball game, he would turn us down. His sinful predilections were making him depressed. He would pray and pray for release from the "*little errands that are connected with that old way of life,*" but he never felt free of them. In fear of failure, he rarely even ventured from his room.

Thank God, something finally broke through my friend's thinking, and he relaxed and embraced the fact that as a human he would indeed sin. He realized that he'd been "raised from the dead." There were things he could do to avoid sinning, but God accepted him through Christ as righteous, and wanted to love him and use him just as he was.

This sincere believer had become so obsessed with living a sinless life, swatting down every sinful thought with a holy smack, that he could never get around to throwing himself *"wholeheartedly and full-time . . . into God's way of doing things."*

I don't mean to minimize the power of sin. Being a follower of Christ requires a total change of thinking, a turning around from back to front. It means letting go of every last vestige, habit, or hint of sin. It requires that we stop hanging around places or people or things that pull our focus away from God's ways.

But the emphasis we give to our efforts of faith can make all the difference in our fulfillment and effectiveness and joy. We can't possibly do it in our own power. That's why God has given us the Holy Spirit: to sustain, strengthen, and guide us.

I have a feeling that if we would focus on a vibrant, wholehearted, all-out pursuit of God, the sin part would take care of itself.

So, don't hold back. Don't let anything, even sin, hold you back. Throw yourself fully and unreservedly into God's arms, into God's way of life.

God, guide me into a more mature understanding of sin and its place in my life. Help me to accept my humanity but rely on your power. I want to leap into your will for me, wholeheartedly pursuing your radical way of life. Without looking back. Amen. ■

43

LIVE ABUNDANTLY

. . . BY TRUSTING JESUS IN LIFE'S STORMS

> Awake now, he told the wind to pipe down and said to the sea, "Quiet! Settle down!" The wind ran out of breath; the sea became smooth as glass. Jesus reprimanded the disciples: "Why are you such cowards? Don't you have any faith at all?" (Mark 4:39-40)

SOME YEARS AGO, A friend of mine from church invited me and another fellow to spend a few hours relaxing on his new sailboat on Lake Lanier, north of Atlanta. I knew nothing about sailing, but the other two did, so I just went along for the ride. It was a peaceful, balmy summer's eve. Several boats were out enjoying the gentle breezes and the glory of the green hills falling into the man-made lake.

At one point as we sailed around chatting, my friend told me to tie down a line. I did, to the best of my ability. I never did learn all those knots they taught us in Cub Scouts.

In a matter of seconds, a summer thunderstorm descended upon us. A fierce wind caught our sails and tipped us precariously over—the mast pulled nearly parallel with the water.

We were about to sink.

My friend the captain shouted some orders to the other "crewmember"—and I got out of the way. "We've got to lower the sail! Loose that line!" he ordered. The man tried desperately to obey, but my knot was too strong.

"It's knotted up! I can't untie it!" he yelled to the captain.

"If you don't untie it, we'll sink!" the captain yelled, in command but still panicked.

The realization hit me with the force of the sudden summer storm: My stupid knot was about to sink his new sailboat! We could all drown!

Thanks be to God, just before we all got tossed into the lake, our shipmate got that stubborn knot to let loose. The captain frantically pulled down the sail and the ship began to right itself. With the sail down, the wind had nothing to grab on to. We motored in to the dock, all of us sweating and breathing heavily.

Sometimes I wonder what we would have done if Jesus had been on board. Would we have been so panicked? After all, the disciples were.

Jesus had had a long, hard day of teaching and ministering to the growing crowds following him, clamoring for him, needing him. When evening came, he wanted to get away from Galilee to the area of the Gerasenes, on the other side of the sea. So he called his disciples into the boat and sailed away. Of course, he couldn't really escape—several other boats followed him.

Jesus, the Son of God, was tired. He crawled into the stern of the boat and fell asleep. It was apparently a very deep sleep.

> A huge storm came up. Waves poured into the boat, threatening to sink it. And Jesus was in the stern, head on a pillow, sleeping! [The disciples] roused him, saying, "Teacher, is it nothing to you that we're going down?" (verses 37-38)

Have you ever been awakened from a deep sleep by an excited, frightened, panicked person? Maybe a child afraid of the thunder and lightning? Or an emergency phone call? Or a spouse upset after a nightmare? If so, you know that when you're tired and resting deeply, the last thing you want is somebody demanding your immediate attention and accusing you of indifference.

But Jesus' panicking disciples roused him. His first words were directed to the raging storm: "Quiet! Settle down!" Of course, he might also have aimed those words at his faithless followers.

The miracle of his authority over nature must have left them stunned and slack-jawed. His reprimand surely made them feel small; it's clear that he was telling them they could exercise this same power if they only had faith.

Lest we be critical of the disciples, let's admit that we are much like them. When one of life's storms—illness, job loss, betrayal, stress—overwhelms us, we often panic. Instead of confronting the situation in the power and wisdom of God almighty, we run around screaming in terror. Hopeless. Certain we're about to drown. Yelling to the Lord, "Help me!" Because he doesn't even seem to notice the horrible problems we're facing!

Why are we such cowards? Why do we not believe? Why is our faith so small?

Jesus tells us—and the storms around us—"Quiet! Settle down!"

The next time you find yourself in the middle of a sudden thunderstorm, trust the One who can command the storm to cease.

Jesus, I certainly can identify with the disciples. At the first sign of trouble, I want to run away. I scream at you, angry that you don't seem to care. I hear your call to quiet, to trust, to mature faith. Give me the strength and wisdom to accept that call, knowing that when the next storm hits, you are with me, and you empower me to overcome. Amen. ■

44

. . . BY LIVING IN THE MOMENT

> Just make sure you stay alert. Keep close watch over yourselves. Don't forget anything of what you've seen. Don't let your heart wander off. Stay vigilant as long as you live. (Deuteronomy 4:9)

IN *RUTHLESS TRUST,* BRENNAN Manning recounts a story told by the Vietnamese Buddhist monk Thich Nhat Hanh, who was being visited by a Christian leader. The two men shared dinner, then Nhat Hanh said he would wash the dishes before their tea and dessert. The visitor offered to do the dishes while his host made the tea, but the monk said, "I am not sure you know how to wash dishes." The visitor laughed and assured his host that he did. In fact, he'd washed dishes all his life. But the monk replied: "No, you would be washing the dishes in order to have your tea and dessert. That is not the way to wash dishes. You must wash dishes to wash dishes."[4]

What a great illustration of what God invites Moses—and us—to do: Focus on what you are called to do at that moment. Be intentional. Pay close attention to the present.

Sometimes that's harder to do than at other times.

When I started working in downtown Atlanta a few years ago, my commute changed from a manageable thirty minutes covering about eighteen miles to an often insufferable sixty or more minutes over nearly thirty miles. I have to drive from the northeastern suburbs to the heart of the city, along with several million other folks. It took some getting used to, and it can easily be the most exasperating hour of my day. Because when I am going somewhere, I want to be there *now*.

But I started learning to enjoy the commute by being intentional about how I spend that hour. I pray and talk honestly with God about what's on my mind and what I expect to face that day. Sometimes I even cry or yell. Or sing my heart out with a CD. Or listen to an audio book. Or make some phone calls I'd been putting off. Or catch up on the latest news with the morning radio news team. Or simply drive in meditative silence.

I don't always succeed, but I am getting better at intentionally enjoying the journey.

It's amazing the difference this attitude can make. I have even tried to be more intentional about carrying out simple tasks, such as mowing the grass and washing dishes, activities I'd rather not be doing. My natural inclination is to grouse about doing the yard work or cleaning up all the dishes after a big dinner with family and friends. As I stand at the sink, surrounded by food-covered plates, silverware, pots, pans, and serving dishes, I can get frustrated and angry and work haphazardly and ineffectively, possibly breaking a few plates and snapping at my wife in the process. Or I can choose to pay attention to what I am doing. To live in the moment and even enjoy it.

When I do, I can appreciate the wonderful meal I've just enjoyed, feel warmed by the love shared around the table, and be thankful for the clean water I have to wash the dishes. It helps me to do a thorough job without rushing to get it done.

Besides, if something has to be done, I might as well do it right.

It's all about balance and focus. We will always have the myriad responsibilities, some we naturally enjoy and some we don't. But we can learn to take them one at a time.

Will you join me in being intentional about whatever it is you are doing each moment? About how you approach your relationship with your spouse and your children, if you have them? Your friendships; your colleagues at work; your church life?

Be alert. Keep close watch. Stay vigilant. God has something for you to do today, right now.

God, you have called me to fulfill various responsibilities. Help me do so with intentionality, balance, and focus. Help me give every task my utmost. You didn't hold back your love and grace, and I don't want to hold anything back either. Amen. ■

45

LIVE ABUNDANTLY

. . . BY BEING CARELESS IN GOD'S CARE

"If you decide for God, living a life of God-worship, it follows that you don't fuss about what's on the table at mealtimes or whether the clothes in your closet are in fashion. There is far more to your life than the food you put in your stomach, more to your outer appearance than the clothes you hang on your body. Look at the birds, free and unfettered, not tied down to a job description, careless in the care of God. And you count far more to him than birds." (Matthew 6:25-26)

OUR CONSUMER-ORIENTED SOCIETY saturates us with messages about what we should look like, dress like, eat like, feel like, be like. Should we purchase name brand clothing or check out the sales at the discount store?

Meanwhile, in other parts of the world, many are wondering where their next meal is coming from.

To all of us around the world, Jesus speaks these shocking words:

Don't fuss.

Don't worry.

Don't even think about it.

That's not your responsibility. God will take care of you. While you're burning up so much time and energy fretting about the things of life, you're avoiding the real issues.

"There is far more to your life" than food and clothing, Jesus points out. If you have decided for God, if you have chosen to live a "life of God-worship," then get your priorities straight.

What are those priorities?

- Worshiping God.
- Serving others who don't have the food or clothing they need.
- Reaching out to someone in deep emotional distress with words of comfort and hope and understanding.
- Helping out with the needs of those who can't care for themselves because of illness or physical challenges.
- Speaking truth to power, encouraging those in authority to open their eyes and hearts to unmet needs in your community.
- Visiting those in prison.
- Providing for widows and orphans.
- Offering the bread of life to someone whose life seems out of control and hopeless.
- Living a life marked by justice and mercy and humility.

The list could go on and on. But just think what you could do for God if you would trust Jesus to meet all your needs—if you were set free to serve in Jesus' name. It's just basic Christianity.

Jesus beckons you to *"look at the birds, free and unfettered, not tied down to a job description, careless in the care of God."*

Careless in the care of God.

Wouldn't you like to live that way? To feel that carelessness in your soul? To be able to share a foolishly lavish love and care for others in need around you? To experience unfettered, unrestricted freedom from worry, from the myriad details of making your life appear as acceptable to others as possible?

Look to the birds. God takes care of them, giving them everything they need to be free birds. And you are worth so much more to God than birds!

God yearns that you, like those birds, would let go of the anxiety that keeps you from being all God created you to be. And fly.

Jesus, I confess I get all tied up in my concerns about life here and now. Help me to reset my priorities, to clear out my muddled, self-consumed mind, and to love and serve abundantly and lavishly today. Amen. ■

46

LIVE ABUNDANTLY

. . . BY STEPPING OUT BOLDLY

> Peter, suddenly bold, said, "Master, if it's really you, call me to come to you on the water."
>
> He said, "Come ahead."
>
> Jumping out of the boat, Peter walked on the water to Jesus. (Matthew 14:28-29)

WHILE FISHING, THE DISCIPLES caught sight of something bizarre. Their Teacher was coming toward them.

Walking.

On the water.

Peter was "suddenly bold," yet he still had some doubts: *"Master, if it's really you . . . "* After all, Peter's companions thought it was a ghost coming toward them on the water. Sure, it looked like Jesus, but—was he really walking on the water?

So Peter put this apparition coming toward him to the test: "Call me to come to you on the water."

Whatever Peter's motive in asking, Jesus' response to him was, well, so "Jesus." Simple. Clear. Direct. Reassuring. Accepting.

"Come ahead."

Could Jesus be saying the same thing to you? Is he beckoning you into unknown waters? You've wanted to step out of the boat of safety and security, the boat of the status quo, and go for what God is calling you to. You even feel a boldness bubble up at unexpected times, and you so want to do something seemingly extraordinary for Jesus.

And yet, you wonder, *Is it really you, Lord?*

But Jesus still says, "Come ahead."

Once Jesus answered Peter's question, Peter didn't hesitate. He didn't consider the odds. He didn't calculate the chances. He didn't ponder the laws of physics.

He jumped. And walked toward his loving, beckoning friend.

Oh, if only the story would end right there. Wouldn't you feel more ready to jump out too, if you knew Peter ran around the fishing boat while his shocked brothers witnessed the impossible before their very eyes?

Alas, the next two verses reveal what happened:

> But when he looked down at the waves churning beneath his feet, he lost his nerve and started to sink. He cried, "Master, save me!"
>
> Jesus didn't hesitate. He reached down and grabbed his hand. Then he said, "Faint-heart, what got into you?" (verses 30-31)

You probably know that feeling. I know I do. You clearly hear God's call, but then so-called "reality" sets in and slaps you sideways. *Wait a minute*, you think. *This can't be right! I can't be doing this! I'm not strong enough or wise enough or gifted enough or called enough to be doing this! Who do I think I am anyway?*

Jesus' response to Peter gives us insight into the way he will respond to us. He didn't let Peter drown. Instead, he grabbed him and pulled him up. You can almost hear Jesus chuckle as he gently chides his friend and follower.

In those times when you doubt, when you are sinking beneath the waves, Jesus says the same to you: "Faint-heart, what got into you?"

What might happen if you took that first step out of your boat toward your Savior and kept your eyes locked on him? What's the worst that could happen?

So what if you get a little wet? Jesus is there. Pulling you up.

Jesus, you beckon me to the waters of abundant living, coaxing me to risk stepping out of my familiar security. You stand there waiting for me. Can I come to you? Can I trust you? Dare I take a step of faith? Amen. ■

47

. . . BY KEEPING FUELED AND AFLAME

Don't burn out; keep yourselves fueled and aflame. Be alert servants of the Master, cheerfully expectant. Don't quit in hard times; pray all the harder. (Romans 12:11-12)

MANY YEARS AGO, I hit a wall. I had reached a point where my work life just wasn't working for me. The heavy, stressful responsibilities kept me away from my wife and young children far too many hours.

The problems and frustrations and disconnects I experienced in my job began to affect my faith. Was I really serving God? Was God the kind of God who would require such exhausting service "for the cause"?

I believe God was using that situation to call me to move on—not only to a different place of work, but to a different place in my faith. The door suddenly opened wide for another opportunity, one that challenged and blessed me for many years.

Burnout challenged my faith, but my wrestling and questions helped me grow and mature in my understanding of my calling. Doubt deepened my faith. I'm not sure this would have ever happened if I had stayed in that job. Oh, it took some time to lick my wounds and rebuild my faith and learn to serve God freely and willingly and lovingly again. But I moved on.

Now, years later, I find myself in another job, wanting to give all of myself to managing it effectively and reaching people through it, and God's warning through this passage is fresh to me. The last thing I want to do is burn out.

Yes, I want to live full-force for God, responsive to the Spirit's guidance, purified in the crucible of real faith. But I don't want to run out of spiritual fuel.

The key to avoiding burnout, this passage reminds us, is depending on God's power to keep us fueled and aflame. To remember, as the saying goes, "There is a God, and he's not you." Such humble awareness keeps us from working out of our own strength and wisdom rather than God's.

We avoid burnout by keeping in touch with God. We can't just go through the motions of attending worship services, reading devotional materials, and praying the usual prayers; we must intentionally maintain the connection. We must meditate on God's Word, praying honestly and frequently and serving others genuinely and spontaneously.

So when your circumstances bite you and the going gets tough, don't give up. Expect that you will have times like that, and roll with them—and stay connected to God. But also be sensitive to those times when God may be calling you to move on.

Simple advice, but hard to practice—because we think we know so much better than God.

It's not easy to give up our self-assured, self-confident, prideful attitudes and be expectant, empowered, alert servants of the Master.

Let's work on that today.

God, there is a fine line between doing right things in my power and in yours. One leads to self-destruction and burnout. The other brings cheerful energy and fulfillment. I know which path I want to follow. Give me the discernment I need to keep following it, realizing when I wander off in my own power. Fuel me with your presence so I can keep burning for you without burning out. Amen. ■

48

. . . BY REMEMBERING WHAT GOD HAS DONE

GOD said to Moses, "Write this up as a reminder to Joshua, to keep it before him, because I will most certainly wipe the very memory of Amalek off the face of the Earth." (Exodus 17:14)

IN MY BASEMENT, INSIDE a big plastic bin, I keep one or two dozen journals of various types and sizes and binding styles. Occasionally I pull one out and read a few pages. Memories flood my brain as I reread my notes from a day some years earlier.

My wife, Bonnie, encouraged me to start keeping a journal when she gave me a blank book for my birthday a decade and a half ago.

Bonnie wrote this inscription in the journal:

To my loving husband on his 37th birthday—may this be a gift that is healing and life-giving.

It took me another week before I finally put pen to the somewhat overwhelmingly blank pages to write the following:

Thursday, 7:00 A.M.

My new journal beckons, an empty, gaping hole waiting to be filled—with words, feelings, prayers—symbolic of the gaping hole in my life also waiting to be filled. A small step, a simple act of applying pen to paper, intended to be a first step in a journey that promises to be difficult yet rewarding, a journey that God only knows where it leads. And though I still trust God in that, I still fear it. . . . Small steps: carving out more time in the morning to meditate, write, ponder, pray. I have come to a precipice, and stand in confusion and fear. Do I retrace my steps safely backward? Do I take the rocky path less traveled? Do I jump, not sure whether I have a parachute or not? Or do I just stand there, immobilized, frozen? Today I stand there, but I feel I have turned toward the rocky path. My foot is extended. . . .

God, give me insight. I am so rusty, so crusty, so tired. Freedom beckons . . . the freedom of a life lived in the Spirit, in honesty and openness, in truly understanding oneself. I am ready to take a step, I think, but which way?

"The steps of a righteous man are ordained."

I read those words today and feel a sublime detachment. Not that much has changed in my life on the surface. I'm still married with children. Oh, my job is different, I live in a different house, my kids are grown, my daughter has given us a grandson, and I have a different set of friends.

Yet, I feel more settled in my trust in God. I can see areas where I have grown. I'm still in desperate need of God's grace and mercy, and yet I can see that I'm much further down the path because of God's loving and generous beckoning to me.

I'm sure of my growth because of my journal. It reminds me of the ways I've grown spiritually, how God has honed my heart—often a painful process. My journal also reminds me that I am still in the process of learning to live as God wants me to live.

Years ago God told Moses to write down what God had done

for Israel for similar reasons. Israel had defeated the Amalekites in the power of God. As long as Moses kept his arms stretched out over the battlefield—assisted by Aaron and Hur who held up his hands—Israel kept winning.

After the battle was won, God directed Moses to write what had happened on a scroll, in order for Joshua, and all Israel, to remember it. We can still read the account today in the Scriptures. It demonstrates to us that God is faithful to provide the strength and wisdom we need.

Because I've taken the time and made the effort to keep a journal, I find the same lesson between the lines scrawled on those pages. Thank God I have those journals because it's a lesson I need to be reminded of often.

What can you do to help you remember the things God has done in your life? Why not begin doing it today?

God, remind me often of the ways you've worked in my life, helping me to grow, coaxing me toward maturity. For any positive step I've taken, I give you the glory. For you are the one who has brought me to this place. And will lead me forward. Amen. ■

49

. . . BY CHOOSING PRAYER OVER WORRY

> Don't fret or worry. Instead of worrying, pray. Let petitions and praises shape your worries into prayers, letting God know your concerns. Before you know it, a sense of God's wholeness, everything coming together for good, will come and settle you down. It's wonderful what happens when Christ displaces worry at the center of your life. (Philippians 4:6-7)

IT'S AMAZING HOW BUSY the mind can keep itself in the middle of the night, keeping you wide awake. One after another, life's concerns and worries arise, demand attention, and tumble around the brain cells, causing your adrenaline to rush in fear, which only wakes you further, which only opens your mind to still more concerns and worries—including the fact that you aren't getting enough sleep!

Out of the quiet God whispers to us to stop fretting, and instead to pray—but it can be a fine line between worrying over something and praying for something. Sometimes praying about something only makes us more anxious.

In such times, I often turn to meditative prayer, such as the Jesus Prayer—"Lord Jesus Christ, have mercy on me." Or the Lord's Prayer. Or any memorized prayer that forces me to focus on God instead of my fears and worries. Before long my worries have subsided, and I drift away into peaceful sleep.

A wonderful thing happens when we accept God's invitation to lift our concerns to heaven, and then let go of them, putting them into God's hands. When we allow Christ himself to displace the worries at the core of our life, we experience true peace. We catch a glimpse of God's perfect will, "everything coming together for good." We settle down in the realization that God is working in and through every situation that worries us.

What you choose to focus on, and how you choose to focus on it, is up to you.

God beckons you to choose prayer.

To choose Jesus at the center of your life.

To choose peace.

God, when my brain goes feverish with worry and fear, pour your cool, calming, peaceful presence over me. Help me focus on Christ, beckoning to me with outstretched arms, waiting for me to place those burdens in his strong hands. Help me to choose to pray. Amen. ■

50

LIVE ABUNDANTLY

. . . BY ASKING DIRECTLY

> "Here's what I'm saying:
> Ask and you'll get;
> Seek and you'll find;
> Knock and the door will open.
>
> "Don't bargain with God. Be direct. Ask for what you need. This is not a cat-and-mouse, hide-and-seek game we're in." (Luke 11:9-10)

WHEN THEY WERE YOUNG, our two kids would ask, cajole, argue, rationalize, and keep on asking when they wanted something until my wife and I either gave in or blew up.

If we said "no" firmly, they usually got the message. But if we said, "We'll see" or "Maybe later" or "Ask your mother," they were relentless.

Jesus tells us that when we pray, we need to be relentless, to keep on asking and knocking. To persist.

Jesus isn't telling us to try to persuade God or play games or try to trick God. It's not as though we're trying to wear God down with our persistence. He just wants us to be direct and ask for what we want. And keep asking for it.

When I was a boy, riding in the back seat of our family car while we all drove home after church or some other family activity, I would attempt to send Dad mental commands via ESP: *Stop by Nick's News so you can buy me the latest comic books . . . let's go to Nick's News . . . we must stop by Nick's News . . . Nick's News.*

Didn't work very often, of course.

Unlike my father, God can read our minds, yet still tells us to spell out what we need or want.

This doesn't come naturally to me—just ask my wife. But over the years I have become much better at asking for what I want instead of beating around the bush, hinting, hoping someone will figure out what I need without my having to say it, and then passive-aggressively punishing the other person for not reading my mind.

I'm often amazed by what happens when I ask for what I need—boldly, directly, and clearly. Without dancing around it or pretending I'm asking for something else. Things happen!

That's Jesus' point, even when it comes to prayer.

Oh, God's answer may be "No." Or it may be "We'll see."

But unless you are bold enough to ask, you'll never get to "Yes."

Jesus, you model for us an honesty and boldness that I would love to see in my own life. I want this. I'm asking directly for it. I will keep asking for it, seeking it, knocking at the door of heaven for it. Because it's the way you've called me to live. Thank you for the challenge. Amen. ■

51

LIVE ABUNDANTLY

. . . BY LETTING GOD BRING OUT YOUR BEST

> Don't become so well-adjusted to your culture that you fit into it without even thinking. Instead, fix your attention on God. You'll be changed from the inside out. Readily recognize what he wants from you, and quickly respond to it. Unlike the culture around you, always dragging you down to its level of immaturity, God brings the best out of you, develops well-formed maturity in you. (Romans 12:2)

GOD WHISPERS TO YOU to stand out in the world. To look different. To act differently. Not drastically different, just different.

But this doesn't happen automatically. In fact, most of us tend to live just like anyone else in pursuit of a paycheck or gratification or satisfaction at whatever cost. But if we give the Spirit of God free rein over us, something happens to us internally. People can see a difference in our eyes. In our face. In our responses. In our actions. Because God has changed us from the inside out.

God wants to develop a maturity in us in which love, joy, peace, kindness, patience, gentleness, goodness, and humility—the fruits of the Spirit—characterize what we do, say, and think.

Each of us faces a choice every day: to give in to the culture that is "always dragging you down to its level of immaturity"—a level that seems to be dropping day by day. Or to live in constant, open response to God, who "brings the best out of you."

God longs for us to live a holy life, no matter what anyone else may think. To lavish God's limitless love on others. To experience the Spirit's powerful presence to sustain you through all of life.

Those who live like this will experience the closest thing to heaven on earth.

If you want to stand apart from others in our culture, fix your attention on God. Ask—and allow—the Spirit to change you from the inside out.

Our culture might call you crazy. God will call you mature.

God, I'm tired of being trapped by my fears of being different. Help me fix my attention on you and live so that I can respond readily to your invitations to live and serve as a mature follower of Christ. Even if the culture thinks it's crazy. Amen. ■

. . . BY STANDING FIRM IN GOD'S STRENGTH

Truth, righteousness, peace, faith, and salvation are more than words. Learn how to apply them. You'll need them throughout your life. God's Word is an *indispensable* weapon. (Ephesians 6:14)

GOD WANTS TO GIVE you everything you need for spiritual strength, protection, and health. Your generous Lord wants to arm you with truth, righteousness, peace, faith, and salvation.

God's truth can protect you from what's false and empty and unreal.

God's righteousness can protect you from falling into patterns that can be destructive to you or others.

God's peace can protect you from the world's chaos and dissonance.

God's faith can protect you from wandering away from your true calling as a child of God into meaningless, empty pursuits.

God's salvation can protect you from living for yourself, which leads to hell, in every sense of the word.

But God never forces anything on us. You must choose to take this spiritual arsenal and put it to good use. It can protect you as though solid armor covered your body, mind, and spirit. If you use these resources, nothing will penetrate the armor and wound you spiritually. Nothing will bring you down to defeat.

In a nutshell, here's how to apply these powerful resources in your life.

- *Truth is the Word of God.* Before you can apply it, you need to know it, so read, study, and meditate on God's Word. Then learn to put it to work in your life by sitting at the Master's feet, trusting God's Spirit to reveal whatever you need to know whenever you need to know it.
- *Righteousness is the way of God.* As a child of God you are clothed, covered, healed by the perfect work of Christ, who wants you to live a fruitful, energetic life as God's servant. To understand how to apply righteousness to your life and live in God's ways, look to Christ and follow his example.
- *Peace is the presence of God.* By spending time in God's presence through prayer and meditation, you can gain God's peace in your life.
- *Faith is the gift of God.* The Spirit beckons you to accept this gift, to know, to rest in the reality of Christ in your life, trusting God to care for you now and forever. Apply the gift of faith by believing that God will meet your needs.
- *Salvation is the promise of God.* When you turn to Christ in faith, he promises to heal your wounded soul, fill in your empty spaces, and lead you into everlasting life. As you've been healed, you are called to share this salvation with others. Apply salvation to your life by accepting God's healing of your soul.

Truth. Righteousness. Peace. Faith. Salvation. Will you put them on like pieces of protective armor today? Tomorrow? After all, "This is no afternoon athletic contest that we'll walk away from and forget about in a couple of hours. This is for keeps, a life-or-death fight to the finish against the Devil and all his angels" (Ephesians 6:12).

God, you have given me all the spiritual resources I need to make my way through this world into the next. Give me the wisdom and strength to pick them up and put them to good use, for the glory of God. Amen. ■

53

. . . BY DOING WHAT'S RIGHT

"Don't go along with the crowd in doing evil and don't fudge your testimony in a case just to please the crowd." (Exodus 23:2)

WE LIKE TO THINK that only young people have to deal with peer pressure, but have you ever done something because your friends or coworkers were doing it—even though you felt uncomfortable about it? (Hey, you just wanted to be one of the gang!)

Why do we find it so hard to do what's right in a world where seemingly anything goes? A world that promotes pushing the limits, trying to get away with as much as you can in order to be cool?

One reason is our need for acceptance. We want to feel that we are liked and that we belong, so we do whatever it takes to ensure we are. So when others get caught up in mischief—or worse—we sometimes go right along. We do or say what we think everyone else wants us to do or say, just so they'll continue to like us. Before we realize it, we've crossed the line, hurting ourselves or others as the result of our selfish fears.

The "everybody does it" attitude infects all of us at times.

- When we're driving, ignoring speed limits or stop signs.
- When we're doing our taxes, embellishing the reality of our deductions.

- When we're encouraged to go out with the gang instead of spending some much-needed time with a neglected spouse or child.
- When we're writing our résumés and completing job applications, making sure we look as good as possible.
- When we're surfing the Internet, exploring—just out of curiosity—a pornographic site or two.

What's the harm? Everybody does it.

But God invites us to responsibility, to moral strength, in all things. God urges us to build righteous boundaries—even in the little things—because if we adopt an "everybody does it" attitude with the little things, we could embrace it for more significant ones as well.

Some people may not be pleased when we stand up for what's right, but perhaps we shouldn't be trying to please them anyway.

After all, whose opinion really matters?

God, give me the courage to take responsibility and do what's right. To make choices that honor you. No matter what anyone else does, or what others may think of me. Thank you that I don't have to do anything to prove you love me—you accept me as I am. Amen. ■

54

. . . BY BEING HUMBLE

Be down to earth with each other, for—
God has had it with the proud,
But takes delight in just plain people.
So be content with who you are, and don't put on airs. God's strong hand is on you; he'll promote you at the right time. (1 Peter 5:5-6)

WHEN SOMEONE ASKS YOU to work in the nursery or to come out for a workday at church or to serve on a committee or board, do you immediately want to know, *What's in it for me? How can I use this to my own advantage?*

When you come back from a successful business trip, are you tempted to think, *I am so good! My sales are higher than anyone else's. I'm the most important salesperson in this company!*

When someone asks a question about something you think is obvious or makes a statement you disagree with, do you think, *What an idiot! How can that person think that way?*

Most of us are guilty of such thoughts at one time or another. But such reactions reflect arrogance and pride, qualities that keep us closed, unyielding, and distant from others and God.

That's why God urges us to be just the opposite: "Put humility on. Consciously clothe yourself with it. Let it surround you, cover you, cushion you." God encourages us to humble ourselves by putting others first, placing their needs before our own, and reaching out and serving others sacrificially and sincerely.

That's what Jesus did. He set aside everything he was, every divine perk he possessed, to serve God. To become one of us. At the cost of his life.

Even though the cost of humility for us is not nearly so high, it can still cost us, at least in the world's eyes. We may lose prestige, some earthly authority, and privilege. But we gain a pure heart, a clean conscious, and God's pleasure.

You see, humility may not get you ahead in society, but it is the only way to enter the presence of God. It envelops us in God's purpose and keeps us quiet and patient, even when the world explodes around us. It lifts us into the clean, clear heavenly atmosphere. It leads to all sorts of unique blessings, as God promises throughout Scripture:

- The humble are as contented as a baby in a mother's arms. (see Psalm 131:2)
- The humble avoid conflict and discord. (see Proverbs 13:10)
- The humble experience the presence of the Lord. (see Isaiah 57:15)
- The humble will be lifted up before all. (see Luke 14:11)
- The humble will become the greatest in God's kingdom. (see Matthew 18:4)
- The humble will experience God's pure, powerful grace. (see James 4:6)
- The humble will receive the highest and best honors. (see Proverbs 18:12)

And those are just a few of the promises.

It's been well said that one of the greatest paradoxes of the Christian faith is that humility is the avenue to glory.

Eventually.

In the meantime, turn your eyes and your heart from yourself to your neighbor. Put yourself humbly under the hand of God. It is a mighty, loving, secure, and comforting hand—and it is the way to an inexpressible glory.

God, I place my soul, my heart, my life into your loving, mighty hands. Work on my pride—I know the process can be painful, but it is purifying. Thank you that you are willing to work with me on this. Amen. ■

55

. . . by Being Agreeable

Be cheerful. Keep things in good repair. Keep your spirits up. Think in harmony. Be agreeable. Do all that, and the God of love and peace will be with you for sure. (2 Corinthians 13:11)

NEARLY TWENTY-FIVE YEARS old, the wobbly deck on our home was in need of repair. The wood was gray and wrinkled and splintered, and the structure shook when you walked on it. Not a good feeling when you're a dozen or so feet off the ground.

People replace decks all the time without much hassle. Plus several of our friends and my son and son-in-law all offered to help. We could easily take down the old one and put up the new one in one weekend. Simple, right?

Wrong.

Even with all the help, the process was far more difficult, complicated, and exasperating than I expected. It took several weeks just to get a list of lumber and supplies we'd need. Even though I had consulted with two different home improvement stores, we were still misinformed about what we would need for the job, and had to go back to the store numerous times. Plus, it wasn't cheap, but at least the labor was free—well, aside from all the pizza we had to buy.

The weekend we did the work actually went well. With a couple of experienced do-it-yourselfers and deck-builders on our crew, we managed to tear down the old deck and set up the new, improved version. It took three days, but we got the deck and the steps and railings put together handsomely. But my, were those big pieces of lumber heavy. It was exhausting work.

The next week, I called the county inspector to come and check out our handiwork. When I got home from work later that day, I found a big red "warning" tag attached to my permit sign out in front of my home.

We'd flunked. The county prohibited us from using the deck until we fixed several things, to wit: the railings on the stairs were one inch—one inch!—below the required height. We had attached the entire deck incorrectly to the house. We were supposed to use lag *bolts*, not lag *screws*. And we didn't insert flashing—a thin sheet of aluminum—between the deck and home to prevent water running behind the deck and rotting it away from the house. And, oh yes, we had missed a number of nails on the joist holders. On and on and on the inspector's report went.

Frustrated and angry, I called the inspector. "How were we supposed to know the specifics of the county code, so we could have built it right in the first place?" After all, there had been no information provided at the permit office, nor was it available online. And neither of the home improvement stores provided any guidance.

"You're just supposed to know it," he said, as though that made perfect sense. "Or else ask us specific questions." I told him that if I'd known what specific questions to ask, I would have asked him. He added that he understood that the home improvement stores had a policy not to tell customers the code requirements, because in the past they sometimes didn't get it right and their customers would be furious with the wrong advice. So they don't say anything anymore. They don't even give hints, it seems.

Of course by now our construction crew had dissipated. It was now just my friend Ramsay and me, with occasional help from my son-in-law. We had to tear down the new stair railings and start over. We worked the next four full weekends to make things right. I was not happy.

Finally, a re-inspection. This time, thankfully, our deck was officially safe. We could actually have a legal cookout on it!

Not only did the process consume much of my physical energy, it consumed a good deal of emotional energy as well. I can't help but wonder what would have happened if I had maintained a more cheerful attitude during this comedy of errors. If I had kept my spirits up. If I had offered grace to the employees at the home improvement stores and to the county inspector. If I had tried to be agreeable and understanding.

If I had obeyed the wisdom of this verse, I probably would have been much more pleasant to be around; I would definitely have slept a lot better, been more relaxed and peaceful, and I may even have had some fun in the process! Instead I expended a lot of energy getting angry, and I blamed a lot of people for inconveniencing me.

How grateful I am that, unlike me, God always responds with grace and offers us all the help we need. That gives me hope that today—and maybe even tomorrow—I can "Be cheerful. Keep things in good repair. Keep [my] spirits up. Think in harmony. Be agreeable."

God, these simple words communicate a generous invitation to a life of love and peace, the kind of life I yearn to experience. By your power, make these words real in my life. Help me keep my focus on living harmoniously and purposefully in your Spirit. So that whatever happens, you guide my response. Amen. ■

56

. . . BY BEING HONEST

"Don't cheat when measuring length, weight, or quantity. Use honest scales and weights and measures. I am GOD, your God. I brought you out of Egypt." (Leviticus 19:35-36)

THE OTHER DAY A friend of mine expressed frustration over several years of legal problems resulting from a swimming pool carelessly installed in his backyard. Not only did his pool end up sinking, cracking, and leaking, but it also had taken months to install. Eventually a major collapse sent pool water rushing into a neighbor's yard—and house—resulting in expensive repairs my friend had to cover.

It turned out that the pool installer had created similar havoc all over the region, starting many more pool installations than he could possibly handle in order to "corner the market." Many of the projects never got finished, and those that did resulted in just as many problems as my friend had. Of course, the pool-constructing perpetrator skipped town and was never heard from again.

Similar stories involving shady contractors and dishonest businesses appear every day in newspapers and on news broadcasts. Honesty seems hard to come by these days.

Yet, God sets a higher standard for us, one that reflects the holy character of the One we serve: Don't cheat. Use accurate weights and measures, follow through on your promises, keep things on the up and up.

People who do that certainly stand out in today's world, don't they?

How many truly honest people do you know? When I think of an honest person, I think of my former employer, who owns an ad agency. In any problem or misunderstanding with clients, Larry always did what was right—and then some.

When a printed brochure had to be trashed because it included a glaring typographical error (thanks to my not catching it), he ate the cost of reprinting a corrected version—even though the client had reviewed and signed off on the final proofs. When outside photography costs would come in under what he'd estimated, he would reduce the invoice to reflect the actual expense rather than letting it slide and increasing his profit. But if he'd miscalculated the cost and it ended up higher, he would honor his original estimate.

Time after time, Larry did what was fair and just, even when it cost him. Why? Because he knew that God delights in honesty and fairness, and he wanted those qualities to be evident in his life.

Do you? If so, remember this verse the next time you are tempted to:

- Take those twenty extra minutes on your lunch hour, without making them up after work.
- "Forget" to report some untraceable income on your tax return.
- "Borrow" some office paper, pens, and tape for your kids' homework projects.
- Pad an expense report.
- Shade the truth regarding your product's abilities when trying to snare a new account.
- Overpromise and underdeliver.

Let holy honesty permeate your life. God delights in it.

God, you have called me to a holy standard, a more fair and just way of living. Equip me to obey, to be honest and just. I want to enjoy your delight in me. Amen. ■

57

. . . BY JUDGING JUSTLY

"Don't pervert justice. Don't show favoritism to either the poor or the great. Judge on the basis of what is right." (Leviticus 19:15)

IMAGINE THIS SCENE: YOU run into an acquaintance, and before you have barely said hello he starts spewing out an angry story about his college-age son getting caught on campus doing something he wasn't supposed to be doing. "Harmless frat fun," your friend calls it. His face gets redder and his voice louder as he goes on to tell you that his son had to go before the student judicial council, and that he had been judged guilty of violating the student handbook and was punished accordingly.

The college, of course, had distributed to every student on the first day of classes a rather thorough and explicit handbook, a detailed code of conduct with carefully worded consequences for specific infractions. In this case, that code had been followed, with the appropriate punishment meted out.

Now it just so happens that your acquaintance, an alumnus of the same college his son was attending, had become a great success in the business world. You also know how much money he has given the college over the years—not a small sum. And even though he never comes out and specifically says, "Don't they realize who I am?" you know that is exactly the question reverberating in his head. You can almost see him figuring out exactly how much his next alumni contribution to the school would *not* be!

Now let me ask you: Was the judicial council fair? Was the son treated justly?

Of course he was! The council was simply following the rules, doing what was right, regardless of who the perpetrator was.

Unfortunately, judicial proceedings are not always just. The poor are forgiven because they're disadvantaged—or treated even more harshly because they're disadvantaged. The rich sometimes seem to get away with murder, and other times judges make an example of them.

God says that we are not to pervert justice, but to be responsible to do what's right, no matter who is involved. No matter who commits wrong, it's still wrong. A person's economic or corporate or political position should have no influence on the process of justice.

It's easy to point our fingers at others for abusing justice, but aren't all of us guilty from time to time? While we may not be involved in the legal system, aren't we still judges of our fellow humans? Don't we come in contact with and pass judgment on numerous folks every day?

Recently a colleague and I jointly interviewed a number of candidates for an administrative assistant job. We had to judge not only each person's qualifications and experience, but also his or her attitude and personality to ensure a good fit with the rest of the staff. I wanted so much to prefer certain folks because it seemed they needed a chance to make it. But would that have been fair to others who truly possessed the experience we needed?

The justice of God, the justice God seeks, is pure and righteous and perfect. If we want to follow this God, if we want to live abundantly, we will do our best not to show favoritism to anyone. We'll take the responsibility to do what is right. We will judge justly.

With the help of God's wisdom and strength, we'll look at each person as a person, each act as an act.

God, it's so easy to judge people based on externals. But you look upon the heart. Give me a heart of compassionate justice, one that reflects your righteousness. And help me not to judge others—but rather to leave that in your capable hands. Amen. ■

58

. . . BY DEPENDING ON GOD AND EACH OTHER

> Take a good look, friends, at who you were when you got called into this life. I don't see many of "the brightest and the best" among you, not many influential, not many from high-society families. (1 Corinthians 1:26)

GOD ACCEPTS ANYONE INTO the community of faith, no matter what might be the background, personality, quirks, predispositions, race, social status, sex, or financial situation.

We don't always like that, do we? Neither did the Corinthian Christians.

Disagreement and division rocked their church community, and God, through the apostle Paul, sought to bring the various sides back to reality so that they could realize their need for one another, their mutual dependency on Christ, and their equality before the cross. "*Take a good look, friends, at who you were when you got called into this life,*" Paul wrote. Look beyond your posturing and your public façade and see reality.

God is saying the same thing to me and to you.

Take a good look and acknowledge that you don't have any gifts or talents or abilities that make you any better than anyone else. All are gifted and blessed by God to take part in the common cause of Christ. We desperately need each other.

Take a good look and realize that "*God deliberately chose men and women that the culture overlooks and exploits and abuses, chose these 'nobodies' to expose the hollow pretensions of the 'somebodies'*" (verses 27-28).

Take a good look and marvel that you really can't create or accomplish anything, but that "*everything that [you] have—right thinking and right living, a clean slate and a fresh start—comes from God by way of Jesus Christ*" (verses 29-30).

Take a good look and realize that you are where you are, not through your talents and skills, but because God has brought you here, and because your community of faith has encouraged you along the way.

Take a good look, friend.

What do you see?

God, I am thankful for the redemption of my soul and my life. Help me keep this miracle of God in perspective—that it's not the result of anything I've done, and that it doesn't make me any better than anyone else. Help me take a good look at my attitudes toward others, and baptize those attitudes in the love and grace of your will. Amen. ■

59

. . . BY EXAMINING YOURSELF

> Test yourselves to make sure you are solid in the faith. Don't drift along taking everything for granted. Give yourselves regular checkups. You need firsthand evidence, not mere hearsay, that Jesus Christ is in you. Test it out. If you fail the test, do something about it. (2 Corinthians 13:5)

HOW REAL IS YOUR faith? What evidence can you see that demonstrates that you are growing and thriving in your walk with God?

Complacency has no place in a vibrant, wholehearted faith. If we want to follow Christ, we can't drift along doing the same things the same way day after day. We need to make the effort, take the time to look deep within our soul and see what's going on inside us. Such times of reflection and evaluation are the only way to *"make sure you are solid in the faith."*

So take some time regularly to examine your heart. Ask yourself:

- Are there disagreements with other believers I need to work out in a loving way?
- Do I follow the Spirit's promptings to reach out to others?
- Have I hurt someone? Neglected something? Missed the mark in following God?
- Are my habits holy?

- Am I pursuing God's presence through prayer and meditation and the study of God's Word?
- Are my priorities in or out of whack? Am I pursuing things for self-enjoyment? Am I seeking power to build my own sense of accomplishment?
- Am I letting an area of weakness fester without addressing it?
- Is my schedule balanced? Am I making room for spiritual activities, serving others, ministering to others, resting, working, playing, enjoying life?
- Am I on a pathway to growth, or am I stalled or going in circles?
- Does my life provide evidence that Jesus Christ lives in me?

What other questions do you need to ask in this, the most important test of your life?

God urges, *"If you fail the test, do something about it."*

So what do you need to do?

God, give me firsthand evidence that Jesus Christ is in me. Help me to be sensitive to the state of my relationship with you, testing and considering and weighing my attitudes and actions in light of your will. And help me correct the areas that need your attention. I want to hear you say "well done" when I stand before you. Amen. ■

60

LIVE ABUNDANTLY

. . . BY DOING GOOD

Don't let evil get the best of you; get the best of evil by doing good. (Romans 12:21)

WHEN I WAS A boy, the battle of good and evil absorbed a large part of my consciousness. I read story after story about heroes of all kinds battling for truth, justice, and the American way in comic books and adventure stories.

It was all so simple. I knew precisely who the good guys were and who the evil guys were. I knew whom to root for. I could count on the heroes to behave in exactly the same ways from battle to battle. I knew who would ultimately win.

How I wish life was like that!

But it isn't, is it? We yearn for blackest black and whitest white, but all we see are shades of gray. Issues that divide political parties, denominations, churches, even families, are rarely simple yes-or-no decisions.

Certainly, some behaviors can clearly be labeled evil. But while battle lines are drawn over a number of issues, with each side convinced it is the right and good side, many of us step back and see good and bad in both sides.

It's frustrating. But it also stretches our hearts and minds and moves us to pray.

You and I may not be able to solve some of the burning moral and ethical issues of our day, but we can do good rather than evil on a personal level. God urges us to stand strong in the face of injustice or hatred in our own lives and, instead, do good. Do right. Do justice. Do peace.

What would that look like in your own life? How can you do good and not evil in the lives of your fellow workers, your neighbors, your family? How can you do good and not evil in the face of unfairness or need or pain or sickness or oppression?

You and I aren't superheroes in a comic book story, battling the cosmic forces of evil. But we are engaged in a spiritual struggle of life and death, of light and darkness. We are part of the army of God's good work in a world trying desperately to find meaning and to experience love. We can be do-gooders in the best sense of the word.

Every simple act of kindness, every small step you take to offer positive, God-directed help or guidance shared in the spirit of Christ with someone in need "gets the best of evil."

Someday, in some way, there will be some sort of unfathomable cosmic, spiritual battle between the forces of good and the forces of evil. Good will win—unalterably, eternally, and decisively. God has promised.

In the meantime, light a candle in the darkness today through an act of outrageous good. Then light two tomorrow. And the next day. And the next.

Don't let evil get the best of you; get the best of evil by doing good.

God, it's so easy to focus on the wrong done to me, the ways the world mistreats me and messes up my life. That, I realize, is letting evil get the best of me. It holds me down. Keeps me focused on the wrong things. You call me to step forward and share your light by doing good. Help me to do that today. Open my eyes and my heart to the many opportunities I will come across to get the best of evil. Amen. ■

61

LIVE ABUNDANTLY

. . . BY LISTENING FOR THE SPIRIT

"Are your ears awake? Listen. Listen to the Wind Words, the Spirit blowing through the churches." (Revelation 2:7)

IF I STEP OUTSIDE the soundproof *Day 1* recording studio in midtown Atlanta, the noise can be nearly deafening at times. All sorts of traffic, engines racing, horns blaring, tires squealing. Underneath it all is a constant roar, the cacophony of the city awake.

At my home in the suburbs, I hear constant noises: lawn mowers, cars, some construction activity up the street, various neighbors' dogs arguing over some fine point of canine philosophy.

I can't seem to get away from noise—even my thoughts create noise in my head. Worries, questions, things I want to remember—all these clamor to be heard. Sometimes, like today, a song gets stuck in my head, replaying itself over and over again. Thankfully the current number on my cranial jukebox is an uplifting Michael W. Smith worship song. Most of the time it's an annoying ditty I picked up on TV or the radio. I want to unplug that inner jukebox, but sometimes it seems impossible.

I want so much to tune out all the other noises so I can listen, and hear God's voice. I want to wake up my spiritual ears, so the Spirit can whisper the "Wind Words" into my heart because I know that if I don't hear the Spirit's words, I can't live responsively for God.

But how? How do we wake up our ears? How do we listen?

Sometimes I think we try too hard. We sit on the edges of our seats and strain to hear that still, small voice.

What would happen if we simply relaxed? Accepted the noises in our lives as something we must make peace with and even welcome into our awareness? Asked God to awaken our ears and help us recognize that the Spirit is speaking to us?

I was sitting on my deck thinking and praying about what to write about this, noticing all the noises around me in my neighborhood. It took several minutes before I realized a peaceful sound underneath all the other sounds of everyday life—a sound that was nearly drowned out, and so indistinct that I had to consciously realize it was there.

It was the sound of the breeze through the leaves of the trees around and above me. A very slight breeze, but nearly constant. The sound of the wind.

I had to wake up my ears and pay attention to hear the gentle, clean rustle of the green. Just as I have to wake up my ears to hear the "Wind Words" of God's Spirit.

Listen. Can you hear them too? Are you ready to act on them?

Jesus, you invite me to listen to the living Spirit of God within me and around me. But I confess so often my ears are closed up or filled with the meaningless cacophony of the mundane. Open my ears. I want to hear you whisper words of love and wisdom and calling and strength. Speak to me, and let the Spirit blow through me. Amen. ■

62

. . . BY HOLDING ON TO GOD'S TRUTH

"Hold on to the truth you have until I get there." (Revelation 2:25)

MANY OF THE BELIEVERS at the church in Thyatira had gotten way off track, involved in all sorts of wrong-headed approaches to God under the guidance of a false teacher called Jezebel. Jesus beckons the remaining faithful in Thyatira, who were surrounded by a culture of godless depravity, wanton sexuality, and utter selfishness, to hold on to truth. It was a society in pursuit of self-satisfaction and self-promotion, and God's Word had gotten lost in the shuffle.

Sounds familiar, doesn't it?

Jesus encourages those caught in the maelstrom of godlessness to hold on.

Grab hold of God's truth. Embrace it. Hold tight.

You have everything you need to know for this life.

God has given you truth that can set you free, direction that can give you purpose, encouragement that can help you survive.

It's all in God's Word, communicated to you through the Spirit.

Hold on to God's truth. Get to know it better. Trust it. Rest in it.

Because Jesus is coming for you. And when he gets here, everything that's wrong will be made right. Everything that's upside down will be turned rightside up. Everything that's backward will be turned forward. Everything that's empty will be filled.

Knowing that, hold on. Jesus invites you, challenges you, to hold on to what you know is true:

Hold on to Jesus himself.

Jesus, the world is suffocating me with its emptiness, its misdirection, its falseness. It seems to try so hard to force me to turn away, to let go of what I know is right. No matter what I encounter in this struggle-filled world, hold me in your strong arms and give me the strength to grab on to you. And hold on forever. Amen. ■

. . . BY ABIDING

> And now, children, stay with Christ. Live deeply in Christ. Then we'll be ready for him when he appears, ready to receive him with open arms, with no cause for red-faced guilt or lame excuses when he arrives. (1 John 2:28)

RECENTLY THE SUBJECT OF abiding came up in a discussion with one of our *Day 1* radio program speakers. After the recording sessions, we got to talking about the gospel of John—the source of one of the passages she preached on. She told me that one of the things about John's gospel she appreciates is the emphasis on *abiding*—an emphasis carried through in this letter that also bears his name.

But what does it mean to "abide in Christ"? Eugene Peterson captures the sense well: "stay with Christ . . . live deeply in Christ." It means making yourself at home continually in Christ's loving presence.

Saint Teresa of Avila knew about abiding. Born in Spain in 1515, Teresa became a nun in the Carmelite convent—though she was considered a spoiled and unimpressive young woman. Over the years her fervent faith emerged as she instituted reforms in her order. Known for her ecstasies in the presence of God, Teresa wrote several classics of spiritual literature.

Every night Teresa used to converse with Jesus. One evening

Jesus asked Teresa her name. She replied, "Teresa of Jesus."

Teresa was then drawn to ask Jesus his name. He responded, "Jesus of Teresa."[5]

Think about that. Most of us yearn for a relationship with God like this. Deep, personal, meaningful, solid, trustworthy, real. And certainly unusual in a culture marked by shallow roots and superficiality.

How can you build an abiding relationship with Christ?

The same way you would develop a relationship with your best friend or spouse. You'd spend time talking. And listening. Going below surface issues with each other. Spending time together, doing things. Helping others together. Sharing the day's events and viewpoints with each other. Laughing and crying together. Trusting each other. Being as honest and open with each other as possible. Being yourself—no masks, no pretenses, no faking.

Do the same with Jesus.

Do it, and keep doing it, and soon you will be living deeply. Abiding.

And when you are abiding, you are ready to receive God with open arms. Honestly, freely. Without shame or embarrassment.

God, draw me closer to Jesus, every moment, every day. I want to be real with you. Deep with you. Open with you. So I can be ready for all those times you want to do something spectacular in and through me. Amen. ■

64

. . . BY WATCHING FOR CHRIST'S RETURN

"So stay awake, alert. You have no idea what day your Master will show up." (Matthew 24:42)

EVER SINCE SEPTEMBER 11, 2001, most of us have little trouble keeping awake and alert.

The nonstop news channels on TV keep us up to date with every painful event around the world. In a moment we can get the latest reports from the world's hot spots, read the news crawling along the bottom of the screen about other events in the world, and watch split-screen debates on the story of the moment.

Oh, we do keep alert to what's going on around us. We're alert to potential attacks from terrorists. The alert level goes from yellow to orange to red and our senses become acute with fear and trepidation.

On the other hand, being truly awake to reality seems more difficult than ever. This anxious alertness exhausts our senses. We are numb after months—years—of fear and concern and uncertainty. We just want to get away from it all. In many ways we are less alert than ever. Less alert to the ultimate realities. To the health of our personal relationships. To our dependence on God for every moment of every day.

It's easy to slip into a deadness of soul. We've worked so hard to protect ourselves from pain and suffering, from experiencing the sheer razor-edged terror of life in a world that's separated from God, that we have trouble really feeling, being fully awake, to what's true and right and real.

While our eyes are wide open, we cover them lest we see the truth of our needy, decaying souls. While our ears react to every alarm sounded by the media, we close them lest we hear the still, small voice of God beckoning to us, calling us to stay awake, to be alert to the workings of God, to the coming of Christ.

Elizabeth Gilbert's book, *The Last American Man,* tells the true story of Eustace Conway, who left his dysfunctional suburban family at age seventeen to live off the land in the wilds of Appalachia. Ultimately, he amassed a thousand acres of property near Boone, North Carolina, and today he teaches children and adults the ways of nature.

One young man named Dave, desperate for attention after his parents divorced, came to spend some time at the Turtle Island compound to learn how to understand living in the wild and become a man:

> Eustace used his time with Dave to try to have him understand the fundamental essence of his philosophy, which centered on mindfulness. There is no way, Eustace said to Dave, that you can have a decent life as a man if you aren't awake and aware every moment. Show up for your own life, he said. Don't pass your days in a stupor, content to swallow whatever watery ideas modern society may bottle-feed you through the media, satisfied to slumber through life in an instant-gratification sugar coma. The most extraordinary gift you've been given is your

> own humanity, which is about consciousness, so honor that consciousness. . . .
>
> Be awake, Eustace said, (laughing at the very simplicity of it), and you will succeed in this world. When it rains, find shelter! When you're being stung by yellow jackets, run! Only through constant focus can you become independent. Only through independence can you know yourself. And only through knowing yourself will you be able to ask the key questions of your life: *What is it that I am destined to accomplish, and how can I make it happen?*[6]

That's a good reminder to pay attention. But why does Jesus coax us to stay awake and alert? So we can be ready. Ready for him. Ready for the most important event of all: his return.

Jesus has promised to come back. How, when, and where have been the subjects of theological debates since Jesus was here the first time in the flesh. Nevertheless, the day is coming.

Watch. Listen. Stay awake. Be alert.

The day is coming when Jesus will return for you.

You have no idea when you will meet Jesus face-to-face. Jesus invites you to start getting ready now.

> *Jesus, sometimes I feel deadened and detached from reality. It's so easy to slip into unconsciousness. Wake me up. I want to be ready for you, whenever and however you show up in my life. Amen.* ■

65

. . . BY REVELING IN GOD

Celebrate God all day, every day. I mean, *revel* in him! (Philippians 4:4)

IF ONLY I COULD put all this work aside . . .

If only I could reconcile with my wandering child . . .

If only I could get my finances to make some sense . . .

If only I could get my spouse to trust in Christ . . .

If only my ailing parent would recuperate . . .

If only my boss would understand the stress I'm under . . .

If only my car would stop breaking down . . .

If only I didn't have to worry about getting sick . . .

If only . . .

If only life would cooperate, it would be easy to "celebrate God all day, every day." What was Paul thinking?

One thing's for sure, he understood pressure and pain. Paul was in prison when he wrote this verse to the Christians at Philippi. When he urged his fellow believers to revel joyfully in God, he was in shackles, chained to the wall of a dark, fetid cell.

So maybe one's circumstances don't have to inhibit one's celebration.

But, that makes no sense, my mind protests. *How could it possibly work?*

What if we tried? What if, just for a few moments, we set aside our worries, fears, concerns, pains, hardships, circumstances, and celebrated God?

Praise God for the love and mercy lavished upon us . . .

Glorify God for the salvation we can rely on through
Christ . . .

Thank God for all the ways our needs are met . . .

Adore God for all the ways our prayers have been
answered . . .

Sing to the Lord. Revel in God's presence.

Just for a few minutes, right now.

Tomorrow, perhaps for a few minutes more.

Then for an hour or two early next week.

You and I have been invited to a party that never ends. Let's RSVP. Before we know it, we'll be celebrating God all day, every day. No matter where we are, or what we're doing, or who we're with.

God, thank you for your gracious invitation to celebrate your presence in my life. I hereby accept. And I plan to bring a guest or two. Amen. ■

Part Three

God Invites You to

REACH OUT

66

REACH OUT

. . . TO TAKE RESPONSIBILITY FOR CREATION

"Be responsible for fish in the sea and birds in the air, for every living thing that moves on the face of Earth." (Genesis 1:28)

RECENTLY MY WIFE AND I spent a weekend with friends at their beautiful lakeside cottage in north Georgia, right on the border with North Carolina. During an absolutely gorgeous early-summer weekend, we spent wonderful moments together floating on rafts in the cove, walking at night around the lake neighborhoods, staring at the crystal stars, driving country roads and gasping at the verdant vistas before us, and just sitting and gazing at the peaceful lake from their cozy screened porch.

Being outside in God's creation invigorates the senses and helps us reset our overly digitized souls. It enables us to get in touch with the Creator, so we can appreciate not only the creation but also the One who so skillfully put it together for our use and enjoyment.

But as much as God delights in our enjoyment of nature, we need to remind ourselves that we do not own this planet. It belongs to its Creator. We are simply caretakers, tenants who are responsible for its upkeep.

Life on this planet is beautiful and rich and teeming. God beckons to us, welcoming us into this wondrous world. Urging us to experience it. Enjoy it. And take responsibility for it.

What would happen if we took his invitation seriously to reach out to care for the world?

Would we take a greater interest in the environment? In our government's policies regarding preserving it and cleaning it up?

Would we be concerned about the treatment of animals raised to satisfy our physical needs? Or about the survival of species threatened by human invasion?

Would we take more opportunities to enjoy the great outdoors responsibly? To see it, experience it, and spend time surrounded by natural beauty?

What would *you* do if you took this invitation seriously?

God, thank you for the gift of this planet. Help me accept my share of the responsibility to care for it. As I enjoy the riches of creation, keep me mindful of the need to keep it clean and healthy and thriving. Amen. ■

67

REACH OUT

. . . to Those in Darkness

"Get out of bed, Jerusalem!
Wake up. Put your face in the sunlight.
GOD's bright glory has risen for you." (Isaiah 60:1)

WHEN YOU ARE WEIGHED down by guilt or shame . . .

When you are overwhelmed by the increasingly difficult burdens of life . . .

When you are absorbed in worry and fear and uncertainty . . .

When you are reeling in the pain of rejection or abuse . . .

It feels almost impossible to wake up. To get out of bed. To experience life at its fullest.

Yet that was God's invitation to Israel. They had been rejecting God's gracious beckoning for generations and had suffered significantly for their selfish shortsightedness. Now God, through the prophet Isaiah, calls them to shake off that ingrained despondency. "Wake up! Shake the sleep out of your head, the pain off your aching limbs."

Breathe in the new day to the depths of your being. Face the bright morning, God pleads to Jerusalem—and to you.

Receive God's renewing light—the blessings of joy, wisdom, salvation, and restoration. Feel its warmth, experience the healing it brings. This light is the reality of God's perfect, all-encompassing presence in your soul. It is always there, shining. But you have to be awake to sense it.

Hear the Father's invitation. Sense the Spirit's stirring within you. Receive God's luminous blessing on your life, so you can in turn shine on and bless the world around you.

God called Israel to be a channel of blessing to the whole world. In the same way, God calls you. It's a decision of your will, a turning of your face toward the Son, purposefully sensing and receiving the warmth and light. And then reflecting that light to others.

When we open our hearts to the love of God, it softens our hardened hearts and banishes our burdens, pains, and fears. So will you do that today?

God's bright glory has risen.

For you.

God, you beckon me to rise, get out of bed, feel the warmth of your light on my face, and be renewed. Give me the strength to heed your welcome—to receive your blessing so I can in turn reach out and be a blessing to someone else. Amen. ■

68

REACH OUT

. . . TO ACT ON WHAT YOU HEAR

Don't fool yourself into thinking that you are a listener when you are anything but, letting the Word go in one ear and out the other. *Act* on what you hear! (James 1:22)

IF THE CHURCH WOULD take up the challenge of this verse—to do the Word, not just to hear it—we would revolutionize the world.

No charges of hypocrisy could be lodged against the church—preaching one thing and doing another. No more shunning or even ostracizing those to whom the Scripture urges the church to reach out, welcome, and minister.

The only problem is, of course, that the church is made up of individual believers like you and me. So it starts with us. "Those who hear and don't act are like those who glance in the mirror, walk away, and two minutes later have no idea who they are, what they look like" (verse 23).

We're scatterbrained. We research and study and discuss and argue the fine points of the Bible, and then walk away and act as if we had never even read it.

There is a story, probably apocryphal, about a homeless family—a woman with three children under the age of ten—who approached a church one cold, late autumn evening, having seen lights on in the fellowship hall.

The mother knocked on the kitchen door, seeking some food or any sort of help. No one answered. She knocked again. Still no response. The woman peered into one of the windows not far from the kitchen door and saw about a dozen people around a table with a man standing near them talking and gesturing. So there were people there. Didn't they hear her?

She knocked on the window. She saw heads turn in her direction, most of them bearing scowls. She waved at the people gathered in the warm fellowship hall. Finally, the man walked to the door. She anticipated warm support, maybe some covered dish leftovers for her children.

The door opened, the man stuck his head out, surveyed the scene, and said, "We're busy having Bible study. Come back tomorrow," and he shut the door.

The mother was surprised and saddened—and also alarmed as the temperature was dropping rapidly. She tried knocking a few more times, but the people kept their noses in their Bibles. The mother decided to huddle her three children together and wait out the cold night, since the man had said to come back the next day. She had nowhere else to go, after all.

Tragically, the temperatures dropped so low that night that one of her children, a little girl, suffered hypothermia and died.

Thank God, that church was slapped so forcefully by the needless tragedy that they mended their ways, began acting on what they were studying, and soon after launched a ministry to the homeless called "Annie's Kitchen" in memory of the little girl who died as a result of their negligence.

Not a day goes by, the story goes, that those believers don't mourn for the little girl. But they are doing what they can to redeem the tragic loss.

God help us if we neglect to reach out to the poor and needy because we're too busy doing church.

Where God beckons, follow.

What is God showing you? Do it. Stick with it. Act on it and experience the delight and affirmation of your empowering Lord.

> *God, your Word is within me. Make it burn. Grab hold of my stubborn will and soften it so that I will be open to every opportunity to reach out in obedience. I want to delight you with a loving heart. Give me the power, strength, and wisdom to make that happen. Amen.* ■

69

REACH OUT

. . . TO OTHERS THE WAY YOU WANT TO BE TREATED

"Here is a simple, rule-of-thumb guide for behavior: Ask yourself what you want people to do for you, then grab the initiative and do it for *them*. Add up God's Law and Prophets and this is what you get." (Matthew 7:12)

DECADES AFTER MY FIRST encounters with them, a couple of my childhood heroes continue to lift my spirit and entertain my soul. These two people contributed, at least in some small way, to forming my belief system and maybe even some aspects of my personality.

Who are they? Stan Lee and Soupy Sales.

Surprised? I'm serious.

Stan Lee, as you may know, is the co-creator of such beloved comic-book characters as Spider-Man, Hulk, Fantastic Four, and Daredevil (all of whom have been featured in major motion pictures as well).

As a kid, I was enamored with Lee's comic books and their senses-shattering tales of derring-do and do-gooding. Like most preadolescents, I especially identified with born loser Peter Parker, a teenage boy bitten by a radioactive spider, who, while fighting acne and dealing with girl problems, would don blue-and-red spider-webbed tights to prosecute justice and protect humanity from all sorts of evildoers.

Why? Because Peter's late Uncle Ben taught him that "with great power comes great responsibility." In other words, we've all been given gifts, and we should use them for the good of others.

At the same time, Soupy Sales was one of my childhood idols because I found him insanely hilarious. What's more, he was from my hometown of Huntington, West Virginia—a local guy who made good. I even attended the same high school and college Soupy did.

When his New York-based daily children's program aired in Huntington, I would make a beeline home from school to catch it and laugh myself silly watching White Fang and Black Tooth, the wacky door-to-door salesmen, and so many other characters interact with Soupy, who always seemed to let us in on the gag with a warm wink.

Not too long ago, my two heroes seemed to be in collusion to make me think about something. I have been fortunate to "meet" and correspond with Stan Lee via e-mail, and he has been most gracious and encouraging with me—as he is with everyone, it seems.

After I sent him a copy of the *TruthQuest Devotional Journal,* a book I wrote for young people tracing the life and ministry of Christ, Stan e-mailed back a hearty thank you. And he added: "In your card you wrote, 'Our faiths may differ, but. . . ' I beg to disagree. I think our *faiths* are similar—it's merely our *religions* that may differ. . . . I have the greatest respect for any discipline that preaches kindness and charity and love for one's fellow man. Most important of all, to me, 'Do unto others as you'd have them do unto you' is the greatest phrase ever written. If everyone followed that creed, this world would be a paradise."

The very next day, I happened to be reading Soupy Sales's autobiography, *Soupy Sez! My Zany Life and Times*, and stumbled upon this passage:

> Throughout my career, I've tried to be as generous and kind as I possibly could to everyone. In fact—I know this sounds corny—but it's the truth; my motto is, was, and always will be, "Do unto others as you would have them do unto you."[7]

I knew the quotation well. Known as the Golden Rule, it's from the Sermon on the Mount. It's Jesus' summary of the Hebrew Scriptures.

One translation puts it: "In everything do to others as you would have them do to you" (Matthew 7:12, NRSV). But I love how Eugene Peterson has crafted it: *"Ask yourself what you want people to do for you, then grab the initiative and do it for them."*

Of course, just about every religion on earth reflects the concept. But few people have exemplified the Golden Rule as Jesus himself did.

The Golden Rule is not about our expectations regarding how others are to treat us. Or about waiting to see how we're treated before we do anything. It has nothing to do with "an eye for an eye" or "what goes around comes around."

Rather, the Golden Rule starts with each of us taking proactive steps to reach out and serve others, to treat them as we'd like to be treated. It's taking the responsibility to do good for others, regardless of what they do for us, if anything.

What if we actually did that? What if we looked for opportunities to serve others with kindness and self-sacrifice? What if we went out of our way to do something positive and helpful for someone in need?

Of course, none of us has super powers. But if we put into practice even the most basic elements of faith, particularly with a sense of humor and goodwill, we can experience a bit of paradise on this cold, hard earth.

It's within our power. And remember, with great power comes great responsibility.

Jesus, it's pretty simple, really, isn't it? Treat others like I want to be treated. And do it first. Help me do that simple, though seemingly insurmountable, task. Just for today. And maybe the next day. Amen. ■

. . . TO PROCLAIM GOD'S LOVE OPENLY

"Don't be intimidated. Eventually everything is going to be out in the open, and everyone will know how things really are. So don't hesitate to go public now." (Matthew 10:26-27)

I'M ALWAYS AMAZED AND curious when I read in the newspaper about a prominent individual who's caught doing something immoral or illegal.

Just the other day in the city where I live, an upstanding businessman, active in the community and in his church, was arrested for messing around with his children's underage babysitter. His family, his career, his reputation, his very life were all turned upside down in a moment.

Many years ago in a church my family and I attended, the truth about the longtime, beloved pastor's past sexual indiscretions finally came to light. The church's board of elders had known about the grievous sin, but they covered it up. When the truth finally emerged, even after the pastor had retired, people felt so shocked, hurt, and betrayed that a large number of them left the church.

Look at some of the major business failures in the last few years, and you'll see a persistent trend: individuals not only engaging in illegal activities, but doing their best to cover them up. Yet somehow, someone cracks under the pressure of maintaining a falsehood and trying to hide the truth, and the story becomes front-page news for months.

We all have things in our lives that would embarrass us if they were reported by the local TV news team. But Jesus is letting us know that, in truth, there are no secrets. God knows everything. We might as well confess our wrongdoings and live in light of the consequences.

But this truth also has a positive flip side: We are holding on to the most important news humanity has ever known—a secret that so many, many folks still don't know.

It's the secret of God's love. The challenge of living in the way of Christ. The knowledge that all will be well eternally in the power of God.

Why do we keep that wonderful news a secret?

"Don't hesitate to go public," God beckons. Shout it from the rooftops. Proclaim it wherever you go.

It's all going to come out in the end, and everyone will someday know the whole truth. You might as well get started sharing the good news. Today.

Jesus, I acknowledge that, compared to most believers around the world, now and in the past, I have it relatively easy. I don't want to keep you a secret. I want to share you, to proclaim you, to shout your love from the rooftops. Help me. Amen. ■

71

. . . TO SHARE LIFE WITH YOUR FRIENDS

Laugh with your happy friends when they're happy; share tears when they're down. (Romans 12:15)

WHEN MY FRIEND WEPT almost uncontrollably as he told me about his broken engagement, my heart felt like it was broken in nearly as many pieces as his. Yet months later, as he enjoyed a renewed and deepened relationship with the same woman, we found ourselves laughing to tears at the turn of events. Since then we've shared alternating times of joy and sorrow.

That's life when you are in relationship together with God.

Something amazing and powerful happens when we share with others at this level. In community, our joy increases and our sadness lessens. We strengthen each other, teach each other, learn from one another, and bond with each other.

With one another and God those bonds can be unbreakable. We become exponentially more powerful and fruitful together than we are alone.

Yet, sometimes it doesn't occur to us to reach out in friendship. We have enough troubles and experiences of our own to handle. It takes time and effort and energy to get involved so closely in others' lives that they matter to us. It's an intentional act to reach out, to care, to support, to listen, to share with others. While the light times of laughter and joy may be easy and enjoyable, dark times also come with the deal.

Suffering and weeping with others in pain and misery is not easy. It hurts. It drains.

But the wondrous thing in sharing so closely with others in community, whether they are celebrating or mourning, is that those others will be with you in your times of celebrating and mourning.

For this is what it means to be family.

God, I offer my thanks for the family of faith you have surrounded me with, to encourage and prod me, mourn and laugh with me, listen to me, love me. Help me to do the same with them, to be the friend and sibling they need in the dark times and the bright times. Amen. ■

72

REACH OUT

. . . TO GREET OTHERS WITH HOLY AFFECTION

Greet all the Christians there with a holy embrace. (1 Thessalonians 5:26)

YOU'VE PROBABLY READ THIS verse in other translations: "Greet all the Christians there with a holy kiss."

Frankly, that verse always made me—and maybe you—a little uncomfortable. Maybe that's why Eugene Peterson made the translation more contemporary by using the term "holy embrace"—but even the idea of hugging those we don't know can make many of us squirm.

To be sure, our culture is different. The believers in Thessalonica likely didn't give it a second thought. It was, after all, part of their culture to express affection with a kiss. Even today many of the Latin, European, and Middle Eastern cultures tend to be much more physically affectionate with each other and even with strangers. But in our culture we have been taught the value of independence and personal space.

But could we be missing something precious? Maybe we should try to recapture that sense of affection for one another in the community of Christ.

This thought occurred to me recently when I read an article about well-known counselor and author Larry Crabb in

Christianity Today. His spiritual advisor, Brennan Manning, spoke to the reporter about a ritual he and Crabb follow whenever they see each other:

> "As soon as we spot one another," says Manning, "we both jump up and down, run to one another, and kiss one another on the lips."
>
> "Why do you do that?" I ask Manning.
>
> "It's the sheer delight in seeing one another," he says. "When you see two men in public doing that, there's often only one conclusion. But he's so secure in his identity that we can throw caution to the wind. If anybody's got a problem with that, then it's their problem."[8]

What has happened to our culture that has made outward signs of affection unacceptable? Yes, there is the risk of going too far, of acting in ways that aren't appropriate or invited. But maybe we've lost far more than we've gained.

I want to live in the tension of this divine invitation to reach out to others with affection. I want to feel the camaraderie and mutual love with my brothers and sisters.

How might we express delight and affection when we see our brothers and sisters in the community of faith—in ways that are acceptable and safe and yet still passionate and free? Will you join me in wrestling with these questions?

> *God, thank you for the precious, beloved siblings in the faith you've put in my life. Help me show them in righteous ways how much I love and appreciate them. Let them know how deeply loved they are—by me, and by you. Amen.* ■

73

. . . TO STOCKPILE TREASURE IN HEAVEN

"Don't hoard treasure down here where it gets eaten by moths and corroded by rust or—worse!—stolen by burglars. Stockpile treasure in heaven, where it's safe from moth and rust and burglars. It's obvious, isn't it? The place where your treasure is, is the place you will most want to be, and end up being." (Matthew 6:19-21)

I AM A HOARDER. However, I don't typically hoard items of value to anyone else (no, I have no hidden safe filled with rare gems, no personal galleries of original Van Goghs or Monets, although I do have moldering in my basement a few boxes of comic books that may or may not be worth a few bucks). No, the things I hoard are valuable only to me.

They are personal treasures. Boxes of old magazines, copies of all the newspapers I had a hand in producing, school papers and other memorabilia from elementary school through college, more old magazines, journal after journal, mementoes from various trips and vacations, and scads of letters from family members, old buddies, old girlfriends (although I threw those out first).

You see, I'm a *recovering* hoarder. My wife has encouraged me over the years to practice this verse when it comes to earthly treasures. More and more I realize that I really don't need most of this stuff; I never even look at it.

So why do I hold on to these things? Because I want to hold on to the pleasant memories they rekindle. The friends and loved ones, the personal accomplishments, the memorable events, the special places. All those things have meaning for me, and I fear I will lose that meaning if I don't have something concrete to prove that I once had it.

Some years ago I read an article about scientific studies of the brain in which an electric stimulus was applied to various parts of a subject's brain. When the electricity flowed, a memory stored in that particular area of the brain was replayed almost like a movie in the subject's mind—the sounds, smells, and feelings all came back as the scene replayed itself.

I have often wondered what that would be like, reliving a memory stored in my brain on command. It's appealing to me in some odd way—like watching high-tech home movies. Of course, I'd only want to relive the pleasant and joyful memories, and it's not like my brain cells are cataloged in file folders.

Do I really want to relive my past life? Or do I want to live my life now and build new memories for the future and for eternity?

By holding on to such existential ephemera, I am in a sense forcing myself to look backward, to keep my mind and my heart in the past. This tendency can keep me from being in the present, reaching out to those around me *now*, where rich reality resides. It can keep me from looking forward to the future and living in a way that leads me in a positive direction.

Oh, I don't think there's anything wrong with keeping mementos of a life enjoyably lived. But there is something wrong when we need those things in order to feel good about ourselves. In order to feel as though we have a life—when in reality our life is happening right now and just ahead of us.

Jesus invites us to "stockpile treasure in heaven" because "the place where your treasure is, is the place you will most want to be, and end up being."

But how do we stockpile treasure in heaven?

Clearly, a life of service to others in the name of Christ, a life well-lived in God's eyes will be rewarded in heaven in some way that will blow our puny human minds. If we were to take Jesus seriously about his admonitions to reach out to the sick and the prisoners and the naked and the hungry, we would find out more fully what this can ultimately mean to us in heaven.

In the meantime, where do you most want to be? In a past you cannot relive or change? Or creating a life in the now—a servant's life that will help you prepare the way for an eternity with God that forever celebrates a life well-lived?

Excuse me, but I have a basement to clean out.

Jesus, help me to refocus my attention on the treasures of heaven instead of the silly, useless, and unreal ephemera of this life. Give me the insight, the strength, the boldness to make generous deposits to my heavenly stockpile today. Amen. ■

74

. . . TO THE LOST AND CONFUSED

"Go to the lost, confused people right here in the neighborhood. Tell them that the kingdom is here. Bring health to the sick. Raise the dead. Touch the untouchables. Kick out the demons. You have been treated generously, so live generously.

"Don't think you have to put on a fund-raising campaign before you start. You don't need a lot of equipment. *You* are the equipment, and all you need to keep that going is three meals a day. Travel light.

"When you enter a town or village, don't insist on staying in a luxury inn. Get a modest place with some modest people, and be content there until you leave.

"When you knock on a door, be courteous in your greeting. If they welcome you, be gentle in your conversation. If they don't welcome you, quietly withdraw. Don't make a scene. Shrug your shoulders and be on your way. You can be sure that on Judgment Day they'll be mighty sorry—but it's no concern of yours now." (Matthew 10:6-15)

JESUS MAKES TELLING OTHERS about him sound so simple.

Meanwhile, in the church today we have all sorts of responses and reactions to the concept of evangelism. Many recoil in fear from the very idea. Others create mammoth, highly organized, multimedia campaigns—and somehow the clear, clean, simple message of God's love gets lost in the hoopla.

Jesus called his twelve disciples to him and gave them a list of very simple imperatives, beginning with:

"Go."

He instructed the disciples to start with their fellow Israelites: "Go to the lost, confused people right here in the neighborhood."

Know anyone like that?

Go.

But don't make a big deal about it. Telling others about Jesus is just something you do while you go about your life.

Just do what you normally do, and be open to the possibilities to say a word, to perform an act of kindness, to offer a listening ear, to share the love and presence of God. Pay attention to the Spirit's inner prompting about who around you may need a word of encouragement or help. Be clear and simple and direct about God's presence with them right now. Meet any needs you can, and be open to receiving others' hospitality in turn. Don't make a big deal about those who don't want to listen to you, just walk away.

A friend of mine was able to do this in a unique way on a mission trip to Argentina. The team wanted to put these verses into practice—to enter a village and seek out those who might be open to their message of God's salvation. They stayed in simple homes and ate whatever was given to them. They asked everyone they met, "How can I pray for you?" That question always seemed to open the door to a conversation and for the Spirit to work.

These encounters revolutionized my friend. Though the culture was different, the needs of the people in this foreign land were the same as those at home—needs for love and acceptance and hope and faith—needs that dwell at the core of each one of us. When he returned home, he continued to treat people he encountered at work, in the neighborhood, and at his church in the same way he had treated people in Argentina.

My friend got what Jesus was saying. We do not need to go to Argentina to witness, although maybe that should be an option.

Jesus coaxes us to follow his lead in our own neighborhoods, our own spheres of influence.

"You have been treated generously, so live generously."

As you go about your life, live generously in word and deed. Lavishly share the peace and love of the God who has grabbed hold of your soul.

Help bring the kingdom of heaven a little closer to this needy world.

> *Jesus, you beckon me to go. To reach out, to bear witness of your love. What's holding me back? Help me take the first step. Walk with me. Help me to live generously and lavishly—as lavish as you have been with me. Amen.* ■

REACH OUT

. . . TO MAKE FRIENDS WITH EVERYONE

> Get along with each other; don't be stuck-up. Make friends with nobodies; don't be the great somebody. Don't hit back; discover beauty in everyone. If you've got it in you, get along with everybody. (Romans 12:16-18)

HAVE YOU EVER TAKEN an interest in someone who doesn't expect to be spoken to — to ask a question or make a comment? A fellow passenger on the elevator. A restaurant server. A janitor. A grocery store cashier. The person sitting in the pew ahead of you.

When I do this, I feel better, and I think the other person does too. Our faces light up. We chuckle. We connect.

This happened to me on a late-evening flight about a year ago. I was sitting next to a man who appeared to be somewhat frustrated and nervous. He took the initiative to open the door to our interaction, asking me a simple question, but it soon became an open and mutually encouraging conversation between two brothers in Christ that lasted until after we landed. I'm sure we distracted those around us trying to catch some shut-eye.

He was heading for Florida, through Atlanta, to meet up with his wife and young daughter, who had flown down earlier to be with a family member who had fallen seriously ill. He had been delayed due to a major setback at his work. He was not having a good day.

We talked together about how God uses such difficult times and frustrations. With his faith holding strong in the face of life's unexpected pains, this new friend certainly encouraged me more than I did him. Both our spirits were lifted through the mystery of brotherhood.

Toward the end of our conversation, we both acknowledged that we rarely talked to our fellow passengers on airplanes. I don't believe our meeting was a coincidence. God had opened this door, and I'm glad both of us entered it. We have remained sporadically in touch via e-mail. In fact, just today I received an e-mail from him with a link to a collection of photos from his recent family reunion.

God prompted the two of us, one white, one African-American, to accept this scriptural invitation to "make friends," and I was blessed by that divinely ordained encounter. Experiences like this encourage me to keep reaching out to whomever I run into when the opportunity arises.

I wonder, how many blessings are we missing when we keep to ourselves? How many hearts could God have touched through a simple word from us?

God urges us to be aware of others around us, not oblivious to them. To see the beauty in each person's soul. When we do, our own souls will be enriched.

God, help me get along with whomever I encounter today— even those I might not usually give a second glance. Help me to see the divine beauty within each person, to sense our common human bonds, to sense a holy connection through our relationship with you. Amen. ■

76

REACH OUT

. . . TO SERVE THOSE IN NEED

> "Then the King will say to those on his right, 'Enter, you who are blessed by my Father! Take what's coming to you in this kingdom. It's been ready for you since the world's foundation. And here's why:
>
> I was hungry and you fed me,
> I was thirsty and you gave me a drink,
> I was homeless and you gave me a room,
> I was shivering and you gave me clothes,
> I was sick and you stopped to visit,
> I was in prison and you came to me.'" (Matthew 25:34-36)

WHEN JESUS COMES BACK to Earth, he will go through the painful process of separating all humans into two camps: the "sheep" and the "goats."

Until then, the sheep and goats will live together, work together, play together. At home, at work, at church, in the community. But at some point, the Bible says, the distinction will be made. A holy God demands it.

The sheep will hear Jesus' precious invitation to "Enter," and will enjoy eternal communion with Jesus. The sheep will get what's coming to them in the kingdom of heaven.

Strangely, Jesus doesn't set forth a clear presentation of the gospel, even though this appears to have been an ideal time to do so. Instead, Jesus sets out some clear and surprising reasons as to why the sheep get to spend eternity in communal bliss:

They fed the hungry. Brought water to the thirsty. Provided

shelter for the homeless. Gave clothes to those who had none. Visited the sick. And ministered to those in prison.

Jesus further explains: *"I'm telling the solemn truth: Whenever you did one of these things to someone overlooked or ignored, that was me—you did it to me"* (verse 40).

Does this passage make you feel uncomfortable? It does me.

Oh, I've done a few things like that. I spent the night in a homeless family shelter, once. I've served in a soup kitchen a few times. I've given my used clothes to the Salvation Army and Goodwill—after they didn't sell at our garage sales.

Yet Jesus uses these descriptions to explain who's going to make it to heaven.

Is he saying that those sorts of self-sacrificial acts—not unlike his own on the cross—are representative of those whose lives have truly been touched by his healing power and grace?

Is he saying that those who truly know Jesus and follow him will be involved, not only in speaking the message of salvation, but also in ministering to those who need hope and mercy?

Is he saying that the redeemed—those whose lives have been touched and cleansed and changed and empowered by God through Christ—naturally seek to reach out to those who haven't yet experienced his redemption?

If he is saying those things, then where am I in the process?

Jesus doesn't charge the goats with doing anything wrong. In fact, they did nothing—and that was the problem. They were so focused on their own lives, their own comfort and needs and desires, that they ignored the crying needs that surrounded them.

Each crying need has a face, and each of those faces is Christ's face.

By ignoring those needs, we are ignoring Christ.

To enter into the eternal realm, we must serve those in need—

even those with disgusting, nasty, get-your-hands-dirty kinds of needs.

When we do, we come face-to-face with Christ himself.

Jesus, help me see your face in every single person I come across today. Use me to help meet somebody's need today. Keep me alert to the opportunities you bring before me continually. Amen. ■

REACH OUT

. . . TO LOVE YOUR ENEMIES

"I tell you, love your enemies. Help and give without expecting a return. You'll never—I promise—regret it. Live out this God-created identity the way our Father lives toward us, generously and graciously, even when we're at our worst. Our Father is kind; you be kind." (Luke 6:35-36)

SEVERAL TIMES A YEAR my wife and I visit with our dear friends Harold and Kathryn. Recently they spent the night in our home while in Atlanta, and we talked for hours sitting on our back deck, which they had helped us build some months earlier.

During the course of the conversation, my wife and I were complaining about our dog, Toby. He is a sweet, well-trained dog, but he has some aggravating habits and sheds enough hair to drive us to distraction at times. Over the years, he's become increasingly frightened of thunderstorms, so even when it simply threatens to shower he goes berserk, chewing and scratching up doorways and walls in an effort to hide or escape.

Life would be so much simpler without him, we thought.

But our friends told us about a dog they had had for many years, a gray terrier mutt named John that their kids had brought home one day. After their kids had moved out, Harold and Kathryn waited patiently for years for John to die a natural death. The dog stubbornly held on for fifteen years, driving them nuts with his frustrating dog habits.

Time after time after time John would chew through the pickets of their backyard fence and escape. Harold would conceive new ways to block his access to the fence, but John would always find a way around them, resulting in numerous tickets from the city's animal control officer. One day a policeman showed up at Harold's office, threatening to take him to jail for "contempt of court." Apparently Harold had inadvertently forgotten to pay one of the animal control citations issued when John had rampaged through the neighborhood.

It would have been so easy to decide to get rid of that dog, they told us. "But John taught us a lot about loving," Kathryn said. "After all, love is a choice and we made the conscious decision to love John. We learned how to put up with his bad habits and appreciate his loyal love for us. And before long, we were applying this concept of deciding to love to other people, including ourselves. John changed our lives."

If I didn't have to apply it to my relationship with my own dog, I would think that was a pretty powerful story.

Love *is* a choice. It's a hard choice. It's messy and painful and comes with all sorts of ramifications and reactions and difficult situations in its wake.

But God chose to love us.

No matter what, God continues to choose to love us, and there is no changing the divine mind. We're messy. We're a pain. We struggle against that love because it makes no sense to us.

Nevertheless, God loves us "generously and graciously." Forever.

That's nice, but it doesn't stop there. Jesus calls us to love others in this same way. Not just annoying dogs—everyone. We're to reach out and love the neighbors we just can't seem to get along with, the coworkers who keep stabbing us in the back with our superiors. Those who believe differently from us. Those whose lifestyles make us uncomfortable. Sick people. Imprisoned people. Contagious people.

Everyone.

Just think how kind and merciful God has been with you. Think what God has put up with from you over the years. Yet "our Father is kind."

You be kind too.

Jesus, you make it sound so easy. Just love people. Why is this decision so difficult to make? What keeps me from sticking my neck out to help others? What am I afraid of? Help me appreciate more the kindness and mercy God so abundantly shows me, so that I can be empowered to show others kindness and mercy—generously and graciously. In the power of the Spirit, Amen. ■

78

. . . TO GIVE AWAY YOUR LIFE

"Don't pick on people, jump on their failures, criticize their faults—unless, of course, you want the same treatment. Don't condemn those who are down; that hardness can boomerang. Be easy on people; you'll find life a lot easier. Give away your life; you'll find life given back, but not merely given back—given back with bonus and blessing. Giving, not getting, is the way. Generosity begets generosity." (Luke 6:37-38)

LIFE IS FULL OF conditions. Just look at an ad for an automobile lease or wireless phone plan, and you'll see line after line of indecipherable fine print. Or try to understand a simple contract for purchasing a home—do even lawyers understand what it says? Or read a news story about some celebrity couple's extensive prenuptial agreement.

Or consider your own relationships.

We place all sorts of conditions on others we're in relationship with, from our closest family members to those we simply pass on the street. If we get enough from these people, we'll give to them. If they pay us enough attention or give us the right compliments, we'll be nice to them. If they don't bother us too much, we won't bother them. On and on the conditions go.

Jesus invites us into another way: the way of unconditional love. Giving generously to others without expecting anything back. No secret motives, no hidden agendas. Just giving.

According to Jesus, that means not finding fault with others, picking on their inadequacies, shoving their failures in their faces. When we treat others that way we only open the door to the exact same treatment. Do you really want that?

"Be easy on people; you'll find life a lot easier."

Isn't that true? You know the feeling when you're rushed and overwhelmed by responsibilities and someone brings a matter that needs your immediate attention. It's easy to bite off the person's head. But you also know how much fun it is to be easy, to crack a joke, to ask how the person is doing. Everybody wins.

We hear a lot about karma—what goes around comes around. What you do, for good or ill, will come back to you.

Jesus preaches: *"Give away your life; you'll find life given back."* That's how it works in this universe. But that's not all: Jesus says the life you experience when you live generously is *"not merely given back—[but] given back with bonus and blessing."*

Doesn't that sound like the life you've been waiting to experience? Yearning for God to give you?

It all starts with a decision to reach out and love others unconditionally.

Jesus, I've been so conditioned to look out for myself, to figure out how I can get what I want at whatever cost necessary. Cleanse me of my selfish drive—help me channel that drive outwardly rather than inwardly, so that I can be a channel of your unconditional, selfless, giving love to anyone I meet today. Amen. ■

79

REACH OUT

. . . to Love and Let Love

> "It's easy to see a smudge on your neighbor's face and be oblivious to the ugly sneer on your own. Do you have the nerve to say, 'Let me wash your face for you,' when your own face is distorted by contempt? It's this I-know-better-than-you mentality again, playing a holier-than-thou part instead of just living your own part. Wipe that ugly sneer off your own face and you might be fit to offer a washcloth to your neighbor." (Luke 6:41-42)

WOVEN THROUGHOUT JESUS' WORDS in the Gospels is one common theme: Don't judge other people. Worry about your life, your relationship with God, and leave everyone else to God.

But look around the church today, or take a trip through church history, and you'll see that's one of the most frequently ignored or broken commands Jesus gave us.

Why do we insist that our way is the "right" way? Why do we feel the need to be better than others who don't look or believe or dress or live the way we think is right?

We're focusing on the wrong thing. If we'd focus on our own faults and inadequacies instead of others', we'd find plenty of flaws that need changing.

I found myself struggling with this not long ago while attending a religious convention. Frankly, I didn't believe the same way many of the folks attending this convention believed. Sometimes hearing them talk made my skin crawl. I was in such a furor of self-righteous judgmentalism that I could hardly stand to be in the same gigantic convention hall with some of them for too long. I felt like I was about to explode.

The second day of the convention, I was wandering around the exhibit hall, clucking my tongue at some of the displays that seemed especially over the top. Then I came upon the booth with two people I knew who held much the same beliefs I hold. We are of the same stripe.

The three of us nearly jumped for joy seeing others of our own kind. Immediately we started jabbering back and forth, "Can you believe what that speaker said?" and "Did you see those outrageous bumper stickers at that booth up the aisle here?" and "Oh, it's so good to see someone we can be ourselves with!"

The irony is, I'm sure that several folks at that convention could have said the very same things about us.

Of course, later, God heaped a few burning coals on my head as I met more and more wonderful, thoughtful Christian people at this convention and found them to be utterly charming and guileless.

Sure, there are stubborn, hardheaded people on both sides of every issue. But God beckons us: Don't worry about them. That's their problem. Stop worrying about the little smudges on their faces when you have your own filthy bodies to keep clean.

I've been amazed to discover that many of the people I have disagreed with for so long have turned out to be some of the most genuine, caring people I have ever known. Not that I'm judging, you understand! But it's so easy to fall into knee-jerk reactions to any issue that we never get around to discovering this delightful fact.

Jesus invites us to live and let live. And to love and let love.

Jesus, it's so much easier to see others' faults. To consider my own, I have to take the initiative to study the mirror—the mirror of God's Word, the mirror of the Spirit's presence—to see the areas of my own life that need serious attention. Help me to look upward for your help, and inward at my needs, rather than outward at everyone else's shortcomings. Keep me from being judgmental, for your sake. Amen. ■

80

. . . TO TREAT OTHERS GENTLY

Make a clean break with all cutting, backbiting, profane talk. Be gentle with one another, sensitive. Forgive one another as quickly and thoroughly as God in Christ forgave you. (Ephesians 4:31-32)

GOD INVITES YOU AND me to stop all negative talk. To decide proactively to be gentle with others, sensitive to their needs and situations. To be eager to forgive and hungry for harmony.

If only we would do this. What would our marriages be like? Our relationships with our children? With our coworkers? Friends? Church leaders and fellow believers?

As I write this, I am grieved by the relationship of a married couple I know well. They are good people: loving, responsible, and generally positive. But they are treating each other viciously. So their life is miserable, their children are caught in the crossfire, and they are considering ending the marriage.

Yes, there are issues galore—long-standing problems stemming from all sorts of bad influences, childhood memories, immature choices, and so on. But those issues could be dealt with in maturity and love if this couple would simply choose to be gentle and sensitive with each other and forgive each other "as quickly and thoroughly" as God forgave them. But they have both been wounded so deeply.

Can they make a clean break from all that negativity? I honestly don't know. It's so easy to give up when the situation reaches this point. To run away, believing the relationship is irredeemable. I pray that somehow God will blast through their pain and hurt and negativity with the fresh wind of healing and forgiveness and understanding and love. But will they let God do that?

You know couples just like this. Maybe this describes your own marriage.

How would your behavior change if you took this Scripture seriously? Would you have to change the tone of your voice? Begin building up your partner rather than tearing him or her down? Seek harmony rather than defensiveness?

God encourages you to stay away from negative, destructive talk. But you can only do that with the power of the Spirit. It may seem totally one-sided at first as you pursue this new way of living, but I have seen redemption and healing in such broken relationships too many times to doubt that it can happen.

If you are struggling in the negative, downward spiral of backbiting and hurtful talk, God beckons to you to stop it. Make a clean break. Trust God and make the choice to go for reconciliation, healing, and harmony.

Then watch how God can, in time, provide the balm of love and forgiveness.

God, I confess I open my mouth far too quickly and say things much too negatively at times. How this can help any situation, I don't know. All I know is that it's my natural reaction to pain and fear. But you are supernatural. And your Spirit is with me, ready to empower me to make a clean break from this behavior. Thank you for forgiving me so completely and readily. Help me reach out and share that forgiveness in authentic and powerful ways. Amen. ■

81

. . . TO WELCOME FELLOW BELIEVERS

Welcome with open arms fellow believers who don't see things the way you do. And don't jump all over them every time they do or say something you don't agree with—even when it seems that they are strong on opinions but weak in the faith department. Remember, they have their own history to deal with. Treat them gently. (Romans 14:1)

CHURCHES—DENOMINATIONS—CAN BE hotbeds of controversy. In these times of troubling differences on fundamental issues involving faith, theology, and lifestyles, it's hard to know how people who disagree will treat each other.

Maybe it's women in leadership roles, worship styles, or doctrinal issues that cause division and discord. During such times God invites us to accept other believers with whom we disagree.

- Welcome those with whom you disagree.
- Don't jump down their throats when they say something you don't agree with.
- Realize that they've come to their views as a result of their own history—just as you have.
- Treat them gently.

Perhaps your disagreement is not theological—it might be a decision someone has made that you think is unwise. By all means, share your views with that person, but do it gently and lovingly.

This is not an easy assignment. When we feel that what we believe is right, it's very difficult to accept the right of others to disagree.

God beckons you to converse with believers with whom you disagree, to commune with them, to interact with mutual respect and tolerance, while embracing fellowship with gentleness and sensitivity.

Out of that kind of relationship in community, things happen. God can work. The Spirit can change hearts and minds, and you can honor and serve Jesus together.

Is it possible? Yes. The God who invites you into this sort of dialogue is able to give you the strength and guidance to make it so.

But it begins with your decision to be in community.

God, sometimes I wish you would just tell all of us the right answers to life's toughest questions, the most controversial issues. But, you choose to build wisdom and maturity in us by forcing us to get along and find our way together in your power. Help us along the way to respect one another, to welcome one another, to admire your work in each other's lives, and to treat one another with gentleness. Open our minds and hearts to the way you work in that process. Amen. ■

82

. . . TO MAKE AMENDS

> "This is how I want you to conduct yourself in these matters. If you enter your place of worship and, about to make an offering, you suddenly remember a grudge a friend has against you, abandon your offering, leave immediately, go to this friend and make things right. Then and only then, come back and work things out with God." (Matthew 5:23-24)

FROM ALL APPEARANCES IT seemed as though another typical Sunday service was underway. The liturgy unfolded as usual. The Scriptures were read and largely ignored by the congregants. But the gospel reading included Jesus' bold words in this passage.

The church had had its share of in-house family struggles—maybe more than its share. Somehow the members, representing both sides of a variety of hot-button issues, managed to come together for Sunday worship. Maybe grudgingly, but together.

But conflict would occasionally erupt, threatening the forced unity. Some hurtful words had been hurled. More than one back had been stabbed. Tensions simmered to near the boiling point.

Just before the Eucharist on this Sunday morning, the pastor read this passage again and decided to obey Jesus—to put the words into practice.

It was a definite risk. It could have been very ugly. But he encouraged his congregation to meditate on the verses, to think about how they had hurt someone, and to go to that person and "make things right." Right now.

You could feel people recoiling at the thought. But the pastor remained silent, coaxing them to meditate honestly, courageously, on Jesus' words.

Several minutes passed. Some coughs of discomfort, some writhing in the pews. Several more minutes passed.

Finally, one of the members of the church board stood at his seat, looked across the sanctuary, and walked toward another board member. The look of surprise on the latter's face could be seen from across the sanctuary. The first man sat next to his fellow parishioner and spoke quietly, but firmly. Before long, the two men hugged, wiping tears from their eyes.

The congregation watched in awe as the scene unfolded. Then a second person stood and walked to another member. Three more. Ten more. In the next hour, amidst tears and hugs and warm conversations, two or three dozen folks made things right.

Then, together, they broke the bread and drank the wine of the Lord's Table.

No, this wasn't the end of conflict at that church. But what happened that Sunday morning did change things. Rarely were issues stifled and epithets muttered. Those who disagreed with each other were able to talk things through because they valued the fact that, above all, they were brothers and sisters.

Following Jesus requires taking some difficult, sometimes humiliating, steps. But he beckons you to follow him to peace, because reconciliation with one another comes first, even before coming to God in worship.

Are there folks you know—family, neighbors, friends, coworkers, fellow church members—you need to reach out to? To talk things over with? To be reconciled with? To make amends?

To ask forgiveness? To forgive? Is there something gnawing at you that keeps you from worshiping the Lord "in spirit and in truth"?

Put first things first. Take the initiative.

Then worship God together in peace.

Jesus, I acknowledge the need to be reconciled with some important people in my life. As I follow you and your example, give me the courage to take the first step, to reach out in love, humility, and forgiveness. Restore any broken relationships in the power of your Spirit. Amen. ■

83

. . . TO STRANGERS IN YOUR MIDST

"When a foreigner lives with you in your land, don't take advantage of him. Treat the foreigner the same as a native. Love him like one of your own. Remember that you were once foreigners in Egypt. I am GOD, your God." (Leviticus 19:33-34)

WILFRED WAS THE FIRST African-American I can remember knowing. He was tall and slim, with skin the shade of a dusty, moonless midnight sky. I had trouble understanding him; his accent, though musical, was thick and strange to my four-year-old ears. One of his arms was malformed or had been injured. But Wilfred smiled a lot. He seemed to be a merry man.

Wilfred was an exchange student studying medicine at the university in the city where my father pastored at the time. For a year or so in the late 1950s, Wilfred lived in the garage apartment behind my family's parsonage.

I can still see clearly the shiny new Ford Edsel my father parked in front of our two-story garage. I steered my little black and white metal police pedal-car around and around it—the driveway was pretty much the only level surface on our steeply inclined block. After his classes, Wilfred would come home and greet me warmly as he walked up the wooden staircase to his humble apartment. He always wore a dark suit and a bright white dress shirt.

My folks would invite him to join us for supper on occasion, especially on Sundays, and as we broke bread together, he would tell our family amazing stories about growing up in Liberia—a land that seemed strange and distant to me. After completing medical school, Wilfred intended to return home and serve his people as a doctor.

I had never met anyone like Wilfred. He was different. My young mind could hardly imagine how it must have felt for him to live as a black man and a foreigner in 1950s America, just at the brink of the Civil Rights movement and its often-violent conflicts with the status quo.

All I knew was that he was friendly. And he smiled a lot.

I hope he felt the same about us.

North America has changed dramatically in the past four or five decades. We continue to experience an influx of immigrants from all over the world—not only Africa, but also Central and South America, Asia, the Middle East, and Europe. In Atlanta, areas of town that were formerly home to white suburbanites have become colorful mixtures of Latino and Asian culture. An Indian grocery store and marketplace has opened within walking distance of my suburban home.

Sometimes, frankly, this makes me uncomfortable, like outsiders are encroaching on my turf.

Then I read this verse and think of Wilfred. In the quiet I open my ears and my heart to God's whispered invitation to take responsibility, to reach out and *"Love him like one of your own."*

It doesn't matter whether you live in America or Canada or South America or Russia, you are surrounded by "outsiders" who need to be brought into the family. After all, we're all strangers and aliens here on this earth. We're just passing through. God deeply desires that we enjoy the journey with one another.

God, help me to be responsible to see others as brothers or sisters, no matter who they are or where they're from. Help me love them like one of my own. Because, after all, that's how I'd like to be treated. Amen. ■

84

REACH OUT

. . . TO THE OPPRESSED AND BURDENED

Stoop down and reach out to those who are oppressed. Share their burdens, and so complete Christ's law. (Galatians 6:2)

I'VE NEVER REALLY KNOWN what to do with the homeless. I hear conflicting advice from well-meaning believers.

For a while, I always carried a dollar bill or two in my pocket to give to whoever asked me for money. After all, someone once told me, our responsibility is simply to be willing to give—it is the recipient's responsibility to spend it wisely—on something other than drink or drugs. So, whenever I walked by a homeless person or sat at a red light in my car while a forlorn man held out a battered cardboard sign with a plaintive plea for help, I would hand over that dollar bill. Often I'd also ask for the person's name and chat just a minute.

One time, some folks at my office were talking about a particular homeless man who had been harassing them outside the building's parking deck. I blurted out, "Oh, you mean Ray?" Ray really wasn't a bad sort, though he was a bit aggressive.

But I've since talked to people who work with the homeless, and they have warned me against giving them anything because the homeless often use that money for harmful stuff. Instead, steer the homeless people to a ministry that will feed and house them temporarily. I've been doing that lately.

Every so often, far too rarely, I stop and talk with someone barely surviving on the street. The stories vary wildly and some clearly need mental care. But what do I do? Is it enough to give an occasional gift to an organization that serves the needs of the oppressed? Shouldn't I be ladling soup?

This is an occasional discussion I have with God. I want to reach out and share others' burdens, but I want to do it wisely and in ways that make sense and help in effective ways. I want to do this as part of the body of Christ.

I want to remain open to the Spirit's leading on my heart in order to complete Christ's law of love. Will you join me in this?

God, the oppressed come in many colors, from all social levels and economic strata. Oppression is the universal condition of the heart. Help me be part of the embrace of your Spirit in the world to reach out in wise, effective ways to those who are hurting. Help me to obey the law of Christ to love you and to love one another. Amen. ■

85

. . . TO TOUCH THE OUTCASTS

A leper came to him, begging on his knees, "If you want to, you can cleanse me."

Deeply moved, Jesus put out his hand, touched him, and said, "I want to. Be clean." Then and there the leprosy was gone, his skin smooth and healthy. (Mark 1:40-42)

LEPERS WERE OUTCASTS IN the Jewish system. Their condition made them unacceptable in any social activity, let alone worship. Called "untouchables," they were persona non grata. They had no champion, no protector.

Until Jesus came along.

This bold leper approached Jesus on his knees, but strong in faith. Somehow, he knew who Jesus was. He had heard the stories, perhaps even seen Jesus in action.

The man didn't even ask for healing; he simply stated the truth: "If you want to, you can cleanse me."

The leper obviously wanted to be cleansed of his disease, and he knew he had come to the right person for healing. But he also knew it was Jesus' decision.

The man's bold statement of faith pierced the heart of the Lord. He broke all sorts of laws and customs and social graces by reaching out to the deformed man and touching him.

Then he spoke a glorious imperative to this hopeful soul: "Be clean."

Immediately the words had their intended effect—the man was completely healed and whole.

We don't have to deal with lepers in our society. Medicine has virtually eliminated the disease, or at least controlled it effectively. In fact, scholars tell us the disease called leprosy in the Bible was probably unlike the disease we call leprosy today. We might hear of missions to lepers in some far-flung corner of the globe, but it's just not a problem in our culture today.

So when we read accounts of lepers approaching Jesus, we hardly feel the dread, the deep fear even, that would have elicited. Our immediate response would have been to run to protect ourselves.

Yet Jesus does not run. Rather, he reaches out in an act of total acceptance. His desire was that this faithful man be restored and renewed, and Jesus had the power to accomplish that.

While we don't often run into lepers today, we do encounter folks we'd just as soon run away from. People of different lifestyles, from different countries, with different skin colors. People with contagious diseases. People who are homeless.

And, of course, each of us is a leper in some sense. There are most likely things about us that other people would run away from, if they only knew. Perhaps we are suffering from rejection and avoidance, from shame and insecurity or some other barrier.

First, let's take our "disease" to Jesus. Because we have faith that if he wants to, he can cleanse us.

And he wants to.

Then, let's turn around and accept by faith Jesus' loving invitation to reach out to the untouchables of society and touch them with the love and cleansing power of the Savior.

Do you want to?

Jesus, thank you for wanting to heal me. Thank you for the example of reaching out to others who need healing. I feel your unflinching touch upon my festering wounds. Now, I want to follow you in reaching out to others. Amen. ■

. . . TO HELP REPAIR BROKEN PEOPLE

> Live creatively, friends. If someone falls into sin, forgivingly restore him, saving your critical comments for yourself. *You* might be needing forgiveness before the day's out. (Galatians 6:1)

MANY YEARS AGO, A friend of mine went through a mid-life crisis. He bought a sporty two-seater convertible, even though his wife was pregnant with their second child. Before long, his cries of mid-life desperation only grew louder. He told me glowingly about his new assistant, a beautiful and vibrant young woman, and how excited he was to have her working with him. I felt a check in my spirit, a warning—but I didn't say anything to him at the time.

A few weeks later, he called to say he wanted to talk with me. During a Sunday morning church service we stepped outside, and he unfolded how God had finally brought the perfect woman into his life: his new assistant.

I was the first person he had told. I suspect he thought that I, whom he knew casually as a good, friendly, open-minded, supportive buddy, would encourage his newfound freedom and "God-given" love.

I listened to him quietly for twenty minutes or more. While his wife was at home with their young child, and only weeks away from giving birth to a second, he had been dining out with this lovely young, passionate, creative woman—as he described her. They had spent a good bit of time together, talking, sharing, spinning dreams.

He told me that he felt God was giving him a gift—a woman who more closely shared his life goals, who looked and acted and fulfilled his dream of a companion. He went on to say that he never quite fit into his wife's family. She didn't understand him; she had problems. Clearly God was answering his prayers for a relationship that would be so much better than his current marriage!

Finally, he turned to me with an expectant look, as though inviting my understanding and encouragement to "accept God's gift."

I said as simply and lovingly as I could, "Run. Run as fast as you can away from this woman. This is nothing but trouble. You have a wife and two children, and you are about to damage everybody's lives with one selfish decision."

My friend was shocked and deeply hurt. So! I didn't understand him after all! I was just like everybody else—judgmental and narrow-minded.

I assured him of my love and concern for him, but I also wanted to protect my friend and his family from the painful consequences of some very bad decisions. I encouraged him to at least work through his issues with his wife in therapy.

Ultimately, he was surrounded and mentored by the pastor and several other men in the church. It was a long and painful process, but after some months he made the decision to stay with his wife and children.

What's your response when you find out about someone who is continuing in sin? Do you judge him? Criticize her? Gossip about him? Dismiss her? Abandon him? Ignore her? Shame him? Punish her? Ostracize him? Give up on her?

God beckons us to do something different: "*Forgivingly restore him.*" We do that through counseling, supporting, praying for, and being with that person through the situation.

When you live creatively in a spirit of love and forgiveness, broken people will get repaired. Who knows, someday that broken person might be you.

God, melt my heart with the fire of your holy, forgiving love, so that I will be prepared to reach out and minister to broken hearts and shattered souls. Thank you that you have created a family of faith to surround me in those times, to keep me in touch with you even when I feel like running away. Amen. ■

. . . TO CARE FOR OTHERS CREATIVELY

Help needy Christians; be inventive in hospitality.
(Romans 12:13)

I WAS REQUIRED TO do a thirteen-week internship in a local church as part of my seminary requirements, but my own church was crawling with seminarians. So I found a small congregation across town that had been seeking a student assistant. I ended up serving there as the pastor's student assistant for about a year.

They were a precious flock, and they put up with my inexperience. The pastor made me part of everything he did, from preaching once a month to helping get the newsletters to the post office. The experience stretched me incredibly, on top of a regular load of classes and a handful of part-time paying jobs. But it taught me volumes about hospitality and love and about being part of a caring community of faith.

Jessie, a widow with a heart as big as her neatly kept house in South Dallas, was a member of that congregation. Her daughters, Millie and Martha, both in their fifties, had inherited the generous gene of hospitality from their mother. That year they made my little family, feeling orphaned so far away from home while I was a seminary student, part of their family.

So on every special day—Easter, Thanksgiving, July 4, whatever—we joined them and their extended family for an incredible meal and loving family fellowship. When our son Matthew was born, they were as giddy as grandmothers, all three of them.

Toward the end of that internship year, Milly's health failed. I got the call that she had been rushed to intensive care at a nearby hospital. I still remember seeing Milly in a coma, her little round body at the mercy of a ventilator, causing her lungs to inhale and exhale at a surprising and noisy pace. I felt so helpless.

Milly passed away quickly. Jessie and Martha were devastated by the unexpected loss—Milly was the youngest, after all. One of the most difficult tasks I ever had to do was to help the pastor lead the funeral service, grieving along with Milly's family and friends, who had also become ours.

The year ended and our family moved on to the next phase of our life in Atlanta. But we had become part of that family. And always would be.

Jessie died not long after we moved. But we've kept in touch with Martha through notes, newsletters, Christmas cards, and even an occasional phone call in the two decades since. After all, she's family.

Jessie, Milly, and Martha took seriously God's invitation to be creatively hospitable. They discovered that the joy and love that come from reaching out and helping others, building community with them, and welcoming them into your heart, lasts forever.

Have you?

God, you have ministered to me through so many dear, creative, loving people. Help me to share their love and inventive care with those who desperately need it in the family of God, so that together we can reach out to the world that so rarely experiences love and acceptance. Surprise me with such an opportunity today. And let me be ready for it. Amen. ■

88

. . . TO SERVE WITH PROPER MOTIVES

> "Be especially careful when you are trying to be good so that you don't make a performance out of it. It might be good theater, but the God who made you won't be applauding." (Matthew 6:1)

JUST WHEN WE ARE about to pat ourselves on the back for our good deeds, Jesus invites us to question our motives.

We already know we're supposed to reach out to others, to help those less fortunate, to provide our time, our resources, our abilities for the cause of Christ.

But Jesus wants us to take our act a step further and consider why we do what we do.

Are we performing so that others can see what wonderful Christians we are?

Are we hopeful that our boss sees us taking extra time, making extra effort, so that when it's time to be considered for a pay raise, she might be better inclined to reward us?

Are we hoping to impress that special somebody—the boyfriend or girlfriend, the important leader, the colleague, the spouse, the pastor, the neighbor, whoever it might be—with our wonderful goodness? *See how terrific I am? How helpful I can be? Be amazed at what a wonderful servant I am! Watch how I share the love of Christ with others in need.*

I know that I do. I know how deeply I hope others will notice my good deeds and how many extra hours I put in at work. I desperately want others to see me and be positively impressed by what a great guy I am—with the hope that they will like me more or pay me more or treat me better.

Churches and ministries today have been well trained by the corporate world to announce any positive step we take or good news that might come our way by issuing a press release. We'll send it anywhere we can think of, so people will read it and realize what wonderful people we are, what dedicated Christians, working so hard to spread the gospel. Oh, don't think I don't do that very thing at the ministry I work for.

I even want to make sure the order-taker at the Starbucks notices I leave my extra change in the tip jar. I hate it when they look away just as I am dropping those few coins in. I've even thought of reaching in and pulling them back out to make sure they see me drop them in, but I fear they'll only think I'm stealing.

Jesus calls us on this kind of self-centered, self-promoting behavior. He wants our motives to be pure and honest, God-centered and God-promoting.

He beckons us to serve God, to do what's right. To fulfill the call of justice. To sacrifice and deny ourselves. To go the extra mile.

All for God's sake. Not ours.

And to do it as privately and as discreetly as we possibly can.

Jesus adds:

> "When you do something for someone else, don't call attention to yourself. You've seen them in action, I'm sure—'playactors' I call them—treating prayer meeting and street corner alike as a stage, acting compassionate as

long as someone is watching, playing to the crowds. They get applause, true, but that's all they get." (verse 2)

Jesus invites you to do things for the glory.
Not yours. God's.

Jesus, give me insight into my motives. Through your Spirit within me, make me aware of times I'm doing this for my glory rather than yours. I want to serve you with a clean heart—not a double mind. Amen. ■

REACH OUT

. . . TO GO AND TELL

"Go out and train everyone you meet, far and near, in this way of life, marking them by baptism in the threefold name: Father, Son, and Holy Spirit." (Matthew 28:19)

JESUS TELLS US TO go. When I read that, I realize how much better I like his invitations to "come." To come be with him, spend time in his presence, relax in his love and acceptance, soak in his mercy.

But then he tells us, his disciples, to go.

Mark's parallel passage puts it this way: "Go into the world. Go everywhere and announce the Message of God's good news to one and all" (Mark 16:15).

Don't just go to your neighbors and coworkers. Go into the world. Go everywhere. Go far and near. Go sharing the good news with everyone you come in contact with. Go with the goal of informing and training and revealing and sharing "this way of life."

For this way of life possesses a rhythm. A rhythm . . .

- of coming and going.
- of being with Jesus and then taking him to others.
- of receiving spiritual nourishment and refreshment and joy and then sharing those blessings with others.
- of Sabbath rest and work in the world.

- of learning how to be a disciple and then training others to be disciples too.

All of us move about in our spheres of influence bringing a message. We go out into our communities, our workplaces, our neighborhoods, our family gatherings, and represent something to others. It may be a message of indifference and self-protection, or it may be a message of the reality of the God-transformed life.

Maybe we don't need to make this a daunting task, which prevents us from doing much of anything. Maybe we don't always have to figure out a discipleship curriculum and an evangelism strategy to fulfill this imperative of Christ's.

Maybe, instead, we just need to go out and be open, alert, and available to those opportunities God gives us to say something simple and positive and thought-provoking, or to do a simple act of caring and kindness.

Nothing can happen if we don't *go*.

Jesus, you keep calling me. I keep ignoring you, or postponing you, or explaining your call away. Today, I want to go for you. I need your help. Amen. ■

90

REACH OUT

. . . TO TEACH OTHERS GOD'S WAYS

"Then instruct them in the practice of all I have commanded you. I'll be with you as you do this, day after day after day, right up to the end of the age." (Matthew 28:20)

JESUS HAS TOLD US to go everywhere and introduce him to everyone we meet. But what do we do after we *go*?

Jesus has another imperative for us, another command, another invitation: *"Instruct them in the practice of all I have commanded you."*

Don't just leave the folks you meet high and dry. Form relationships. Become friends with them. Show them how to live. Teach them the ways of Christ. Introduce them to the beauties and riches of a relationship with God through faith.

You see, this isn't a one-time event. It's not a special weekend evangelistic effort to blanket your neighborhood. It isn't a shotgun blast of tracts or pamphlets or simple words.

It's a lifestyle. Day after day after day. Jesus calls us to get into the world and get busy getting the word out. To transfer our knowledge, our understanding, our relationship with the Lord to others.

That means being with people. Spending time with them. Encouraging them to do the same thing with others in their own spheres of influence.

Sound like a huge job, a mammoth responsibility? It is.

But Jesus promises: *"I'll be with you as you do this, day after day after day, right up to the end of the age."*

These final words of Jesus are good words to take with you every step of every day.

Jesus is always with you. In your heart and life, your pains and problems, your loneliness and laziness, your fears and frustrations. Wherever you are, he is there with you.

He'll never leave you. He'll never forget you. He'll never ignore you. He'll help you grow up in the faith, grow stronger in his love.

He will be with you doing this every day. Until the very end.

Jesus, does my life look like this picture you've painted of a faithful follower? One who goes out taking you to everyone I meet? One who reaches out and teaches and encourages and challenges? One who trusts that you are with me every step of the way? I want to accept this challenge, this calling. By faith I do so. Thank you for being with me as I do. Amen. ■

Accepting God's Invitations

A NUMBER OF YEARS ago, when *Braveheart*—Mel Gibson's film extolling the adventurous virtues of William Wallace, the hero of Scotland, was about to be released, I came up with what I thought was a brilliant idea.

I had noticed in checking the newly released telephone directory white pages that there were five other Peter Wallaces in the metro Atlanta area. *What a hoot*, I thought, *to invite the other five Peter Wallaces to meet for a guys' outing, to get to know each other and see this movie about the hero who bore our last name.*

I gathered their addresses from the phone book and worked up an appealing invitation. What fun this would be! We could compare notes about what it was like living with the name Peter Wallace—not that there's anything terribly unique about it, but still!

I sent out the invitations anticipating the great time we'd have when we would all introduce ourselves to our server at the restaurant before the movie. Maybe we could all wear nametags. What a riot!

Days passed. Weeks. The movie finally premiered, but I never heard back from a single other Peter Wallace.

Was my invitation too weird to be taken seriously? Too unusual, unbelievable, or extraordinary? Too unexpected? Too good to be true? Were they all just too busy? Did the other Peter Wallaces have a life?

I have no idea. But sometimes I think we do the same with God's gracious invitations to us. We fail to take God up on them, and we miss out on something a lot bigger than a guy's night out.

As we've seen throughout Scripture from Genesis to Revelation, out of the quiet, God has generously beckoned us to come closer into the holy, energizing, comforting presence of God, to live more abundantly as a child of God, and to reach out to others to serve them and bring them into the family.

I suspect one of the reasons you picked up this book is that you, like me, are tired of playing the game, of simply going through the motions. You want to be with God. You want to experience a genuine spirituality—one that brings fulfillment, purpose, and challenge to your soul. You want to make a difference in the world for the Lord who has so graciously and radically transformed you.

You want to accept the invitations God has whispered to you through the pages of Scripture. A lot of people in this world might consider them too unbelievable, too unusual, too good to be true. Or they're just too busy to accept them.

But not you. You are ready to go for it.

I think the apostle Paul felt much the same way. Consider how his life and ministry changed the world. When I was trying to gather my thoughts for this final invitation to you, I discovered Paul had pretty much already said it, much better than I ever could—and with far more authority. I hope you'll read, slowly and carefully, his encouragement to the Philippians to join him in the adventure of Christian living:

> Yes, all the things I once thought were so important are gone from my life. Compared to the high privilege of knowing Christ Jesus as my Master, firsthand, everything I once thought I had going for me is insignificant—dog

dung. I've dumped it all in the trash so that I could embrace Christ and be embraced by him. I didn't want some petty, inferior brand of righteousness that comes from keeping a list of rules when I could get the robust kind that comes from trusting Christ—*God's* righteousness.

I gave up all that inferior stuff so I could know Christ personally, experience his resurrection power, be a partner in his suffering, and go all the way with him to death itself. If there was any way to get in on the resurrection from the dead, I wanted to do it.

I'm not saying that I have this all together, that I have it made. But I am well on my way, reaching out for Christ, who has so wondrously reached out for me. Friends, don't get me wrong: By no means do I count myself an expert in all of this, but I've got my eye on the goal, where God is beckoning us onward—to Jesus. I'm off and running, and I'm not turning back.

So let's keep focused on that goal, those of us who want everything God has for us. If any of you have something else in mind, something less than total commitment, God will clear your blurred vision—you'll see it yet! Now that we're on the right track, let's stay on it.

Stick with me, friends. Keep track of those you see running this same course, headed for this same goal. There are many out there taking other paths, choosing other goals, and trying to get you to go along with them. I've warned you of them many times; sadly, I'm having to do it again. All they want is easy street. They hate Christ's Cross. But easy street is a dead-end street. Those who live there make their bellies their gods; belches are their praise; all they can think of is their appetites.

> But there's far more to life for us. We're citizens of high heaven! We're waiting the arrival of the Savior, the Master, Jesus Christ, who will transform our earthy bodies into glorious bodies like his own. He'll make us beautiful and whole with the same powerful skill by which he is putting everything as it should be, under and around him.
>
> My dear, dear friends! I love you so much. I do want the very best for you. You make me feel such joy, fill me with such pride. Don't waver. Stay on track, steady in God. (Philippians 3:8—4:1)

God indeed invites us onward. Onward to Christ. Onward to sacrificial service. Onward to eternal fulfillment.

God woos us to "embrace Jesus and be embraced by him." Coaxes us to keep focused on everything God has for us. Beckons us to live generously in holy love, grace, and power.

Will you accept these incredible invitations?

> *Come, family of Jacob,*
> *Let's live in the light of* G*OD. (Isaiah 2:5)*

Notes

1. Hadith Qudsi 15, quoted by Daisy Kahn in a presentation to the Faith and Values Media Member Council, May 2003. [NOTE: a slightly different version appears in print in *Forty Hadith Qudsi,* edited by Ezzeddin Ibrahim and Denys Johnson-Davies, published by the Islamic Texts Society, Cambridge, England, 1997. However I prefer the wording Daisy used in her presentation.]

2. Holy Eucharist Rite II, *The Book of Common Prayer* (New York: The Seabury Press, 1979), p. 362.

3. Holy Eucharist Rite II, *The Book of Common Prayer,* p. 363.

4. Thich Nhat Hanh, *The Miracle of Mindfulness.* Quoted by Brennan Manning, *Ruthless Trust* (San Francisco: HarperSanFrancisco, 2000), p. 157.

5. Karen Johnson, "Teresa of Avila," *Living with Christ,* 4, no. 8 (August 2003), p. 95.

6. Elizabeth Gilbert, *The Last American Man* (New York: Penguin, 2003), pp. 258-259.

7. Soupy Sales with Charles Salzberg, *Soupy Sez! My Zany Life and Times* (New York: M. Evans and Company, 2001), p. 19.

8. Agnieszka Tennant, "A Shrink Gets Stretched," *Christianity Today,* 47, no. 5 (May 2003), p. 52.

Scripture Index

About the Author

PETER M. WALLACE, TH.M., is president of The Protestant Hour, Inc. and executive producer of the *Day 1* ecumenical radio and television ministry (www.Day1.net). He earned a bachelor's degree in journalism/advertising from Marshall University, Huntington, West Virginia, and a Master of Theology degree from Dallas Theological Seminary, Dallas, Texas. Peter served as editorial director for Walk Thru the Bible Ministries from 1984 to 1990. He then was senior copywriter and broadcast producer for Larry Smith & Associates Advertising and Design in Atlanta for eleven years, before joining The Protestant Hour organization in March 2001.

Peter is the author of several books, including *Psalms for Today* (World Bible Publishers), *What Jesus Is Saying to You Today* (Thomas Nelson), and *TruthQuest Devotional Journal* (Broadman & Holman). He has contributed to numerous books, study Bibles, devotional guides, magazines, teaching curriculums, video series, and other resources.

Peter and his wife, Bonnie, are the parents of two grown children and the grandparents of one, and live in the Atlanta, Georgia, area.

"Peter Wallace writes gracefully out of a heart enamored with God and devoted to befriending and encouraging weary pilgrims. *Out of the Quiet* is a warm and wise guide to a richer, deeper spiritual experience."

LEN WOODS, pastor, Christ Community Church, Ruston, LA; author, *Praying God's Promises in Tough Times*

"In this book, Peter Wallace shares with us his rich and imaginative life with God. Served with digestible bites of Scripture, you will find a well-seasoned feast of simple, solid, and grace-filled insights into God's Word. Open to any page and enjoy!"

THE REVEREND DR. VICTOR D. PENTZ, senior pastor, Peachtree Presbyterian Church, Atlanta, GA

"There is a freshness in Peter's writing because it flows so obviously from the real experience of a wayfaring, committed pilgrim. When you read him, you will be encouraged and inspired to embark on your own journey with the Father."

DR. THOMAS LANE BUTTS, pastor emeritus, columnist, author of *Tigers in the Dark*

"God speaks to us in ways great and small and, while we yearn for the drama of lightning flashes and monumental messages, the deepest insights most often are perceived in what Peter Wallace calls the 'quiet whisper.' *Out of the Quiet* is as gentle and welcoming as the most heartening caress of our loving God."

ROY LLOYD, senior manager, media relations American Bible Society